What Others Are Saying...

"This book presents innovative ways of investing to gain higher returns than through customary methods. The book focuses on investing in tax liens and tax deeds, areas of particular interest given the uncertain state of the economy at this time. The book presents the process in straightforward language, with good use of visuals such as flow charts. The author has been careful to insert information about jurisdictional differences and tax laws that could affect investment decisions. He also walks the investor down the path of financing these investments, including potentially using underperforming IRA assets. Also included is additional information on research, bidding strategies, and selling properties to recoup assets. This is an outstanding work sure to at least provoke serious thought about this alternative, and is a great start on getting involved in this investment approach."

Michael Donnelly
Author of *Under the Anthill*

"Finally! An easy to read book that shows you how to invest in foreclosures and tax auctions."

Ben Macht
Surepoint Lending

"Superb, fun to read, and introduces a new alternative to stocks and bonds – Don Sausa shares the secret of banks and wealthy investors. The book guides you from day one to day seven on how to research, and invest in tax liens and tax deed foreclosures. His writing style is refreshing, sprinkled with humor and inviting."

Jen Macanim
Library Weekly

"The average person may not know what tax liens or deeds, or tax certificates are. But when you're done with this book, you'll wish you've known about it a lot earlier! Once you have learned just what liens and deeds are, you will then learn the process of obtaining them as investments."

John Anderson
Barnes & Noble.com customer review

"Seems to be designed for a person with little time to read, a quick straight to the point investment book."

Nick O
Business manager

the COMPLETE GUIDE to

Real Estate

Tax Liens and

Foreclosure

Deeds

Learn in 7 Days!

"Superb, fun to read, and introduces a new alternative to stocks and bonds..."

-Library Weekly

Don Sausa

**PRINTED IN
THE UNITED STATES OF AMERICA**

Copyright © 2006 by The Vision Press

ISBN-10: 0-9788346-8-2 ISBN-13: 978-0-9788346-8-5

Library of Congress Cataloging-in-Publication Data

Sausa, Don.
  Investing without losing : the beginner's guide to real estate
tax lien and tax deed auctions / Don Sausa ; [edited by] Jody Ortiz.
          p. cm.
  Includes bibliographical references and index.
  ISBN 0-9788346-8-2 (978-0-9788346-8-5: alk. paper)
  1. Real estate investment 2. Real estate business. I. Title.

2006939969

Attention real estate organizations, conferences, and seminars: Take 40% off and use our books as fundraisers, premiums, or gifts. Please contact the publisher:

The Vision Press
6900-29 Daniels Pkwy #147
Fort Myers, FL 33912
http://www.TheVisionPress.com
SAN Number: 851–755X

DISCLAIMER: The publisher and the author make no representations or warranties with respect to the accuracy or completeness of the contents of this work and specifically disclaim all warranties, including without limitation warranties of fitness for a particular purpose. If professional assistance is required, the services of a competent professional should be sought.

Author: Don Sausa
Editor: Jody Ortiz

To my wife, Jen, and my baby girl, Kaycee — I love you both.

Contents

Acknowledgements

I would like to acknowledge, dedicate, and deeply thank the various people who, during the time this endeavor lasted, provided me with helpful assistance and loving support. Without their care and consideration, this book would likely not have matured.

To my family who cared, loved, and supported me – my wife Jen, my daughter Kaycee, my sisters Stacey and Trish, and most of all, my parents.

To my colleagues who have helped in one way or another inspire me: Brad Keckler, Jim Searles, Trevor Friesen, Glenna Williams, John Ruch, Jim Searles, Bob Massey, Todd Pierce, Nick Obtenu, and the rest of my former colleagues at TP USA & BellSouth.

To my copy editor and layout coordinator – Jody Ortiz, who worked tirelessly to get through the book.

To Coshi and Eloise, one of the best real estate teams in the nation.

To Master Guak, Master Larry, and to my friends at UMAC who worked tirelessly to motivate me to finish my book so I can start coming back for classes again.

And last but not least, to God, in Him we have the resurrection and the life. To my church family who has always been a source of motivation.

Preface

The terms "safe investment" and "good returns" are usually not synonymous terms, but in rare occasions, they can be. In the next seven days, I'll introduce you to an investment vehicle that's gaining popularity -- real estate tax auctions.

I'm sure you've heard about tax auctions. I've personally seen it on late night infomercials. I usually see someone with a suit, offering an opportunity to get into a new money making system. The setting is usually overseeing a waterfront view or a million dollar yacht or even a talk-show host format.

The infomercial offers examples of how they made hundreds of thousands of dollars in a matter of weeks just by using the "system".

But what's the catch?

First, the $19.95 is a teaser price. You have to buy additional materials, or have coaching sessions that could cost up to $150/hour.

Here's one comment from a customer that bought a real estate "system":

> Purchased the Tax Lien Program for 3k. Have been unable to utilize or understand the program. We have exceeded the 3 day return window and is now being denied a refund. The program requires more time than lead on. We have 4 children and we each have fulltime jobs which does not allow extra time.
>
> We are in desperate need of the funds just for living expenses.
>
> Martin
> Vacaville, California
> U.S.A.
>
> Source: RipOffReport.com

The fundamental investment principles that a lot of these "systems" are based on are actually sound; however, there's a lot of hype and marketing gimmicks that seems to dilute the information. Martin, who purchased a tax lien "system" for $3,000 simply didn't know what he was getting into.

I'm disappointed that so many real estate gurus have used their knowledge for the bad rather than for the good. One of the main reasons I wrote this book is to help others, like Martin, in understanding this area of real estate investing.

Tax auctions are one of the most exciting investment alternatives out there, because you're actually in the action, bidding, strategizing, and researching. It is definitely something to be considered if you want to diversify your investment portfolio.

Like other investments, you can get burned if you don't know what you're doing, but if you apply research and due diligence into your bidding strategies, it's almost like you're investing without losing.

My Promise

My promise to you the reader is to make this book simple to follow, easy-to-read, and useful. From the first page to the last, I've designed it to make sure the information provided to you is direct to the point. And if you can't understand a particular topic, please post your question on my web site at www.InvestingWithoutLosing.com.

Good luck, and happy reading!

Don Sausa

"Only those who dare to fail greatly can ever achieve greatly."

-Robert F. Kennedy

Day 1: Know The Types of Auctions

The safest type of investment is the one that's either secured or insured. For instance, a savings account from your local bank is insured by the federal government. You're relatively secure knowing that the government is behind you. Unfortunately, savings accounts have a relatively low rate of return – usually hovering somewhere between one to four percent. It's as fun as watching snails move!

Though there's nothing inherently wrong about savings accounts or other slow growth accounts, they should not be the main place for your investments if there are other safer venues that can deliver better returns. Why take 1-4% returns if you can achieve 12% or more for relatively the same amount of risk?

Best Returns Usually Means High Risk

The best returns usually come from the riskiest types of investments. In the past, only those brave enough to risk it all in either the stock market or other similar financial ventures were fortunate enough to realize large gains from their investments. Unfortunately, opportunities such as these don't pay off for everyone. While some gain, most lose.

The Y2K bubble economy of the late 1990s was a clear example of this. Even fundamental investors started to question whether sound investment principles no longer applied as people continued to gain millions of dollars in stock by investing in non-performing high market cap companies.

In the fall of 2000, reality hit and everyone learned what happens when you play with speculative investments. You get burned. Dot com companies that were the darlings of Wall Street were continuing to report record losses. As stock losses came in, companies were pressured to perform and corporate executives played accounting magic.

The end result of all the hype, speculation, and corporate scandals fueled the way for a devastating recession. Individuals, families, retirees, and corporations went bankrupt.

Those that were able to catch on early withdrew their investments off the stock market and reinvested into more stable accounts or funds, at a lesser rate of return.

During this time, many investors (like this author) looked for alternative methods of investing their money.

The million dollar question that came out of the dot com bust was: is there a type of investment vehicle that can offer good returns yet be secure?

The answer is yes.

Introducing Tax Liens: Safe, Good Returns

The tax lien investment vehicle is the ultimate blending of good returns and security. Like savings accounts, it is "insured". Instead of the FDIC, tax liens are secured by real estate.

Tax liens also offer a peace of mind because it's enforced by the state government and set in state statute. Additionally, since its run by the government, the rates do not get affected by corporate scandals, Middle East oil issues, North Korean missiles, or quarterly earning reports.

For instance, if you invest in tax liens in the state of Florida, you could potentially earn a yearly interest rate of 18 percent. In Arizona, their default interest rate is 16 percent. In 2005, Colorado's rate of return was 14 percent.

These interest rates are set! They are not modified or moved on a whim by market pressures.

Within the next few days, you'll quickly learn how to participate in these auctions and how to come out with a profit.

What Are Tax Liens?

A tax lien is a statutory lien placed against a property. A tax lien is usually filed because the owner did not pay his property taxes.

Property taxes are the primary source of revenue for state and county governments. On a local and state level, without assessing these taxes, there would be no schools, police, road improvements, road repairs, fire departments or any other county or parish funded entities.

By filing a tax lien and selling the lien to an investor, the county is able to recoup their property tax loss. The investor in return will be paid interest and penalties if the property owner pays for the lien.

If the lien is not paid after a certain amount of time, the owner could lose the property. Each state that sells tax liens has a set redemption periods for repaying liens.

A redemption period is the length of time property owners are allowed to pay the debt after the lien is filed. If they don't pay within that given time frame, the investor can recoup his investment by owning the property outright.

For instance, in the state of Texas, if a property owner doesn't pay his lien to the county's tax collector within the given six month redemption period, he could lose ownership of his non-homestead property to the investor.

Why Do Property Owners Do This?

You may be wondering why a property owner would allow his property to have a lien held against it. Many have paid on their property for years and have acquired thousands or even hundreds of thousands of dollars in equity. So what would cause them to fall behind on their taxes to the point of risking all that they have in their investment?

Surprisingly, many of these situations arise from the simple mishandling of a tax bill. Some also leave the properties that they do not want to simply fall into foreclosure. Whatever the reason is for their tax delinquency, their loss is your gain.

Remember, not only are you helping yourself by investing in tax liens, you are also helping others – without investors, county governments wouldn't have balanced budgets and government employees like 911 operators wouldn't exist.

Are These Properties Dumps?

One of the biggest misconceptions about tax auctions is that the property must be worthless for the owner not to pay their taxes on time. Though you'll find many listed in tax lien auctions as unbuildable, and unsellable, there are many diamonds in the rough.

Check out this beautiful five acre lot in Ft Garland, Colorado:

This stunning ranch property that sits besides the Rocky Mountains had a tax lien on it. The owner was from Saudi Arabia and no longer paid the property taxes. Who knows why he ignored his five acre ranch property – he may have forgotten about it, or thought it was too cumbersome to maintain something thousands of miles away.

No one truly knows the reason why people leave assets behind, sitting idle with taxes unpaid. What is known is that it is an opportunity for investors like you.

(The tax lien on the Colorado property was $157.19.)

To recap, there are two avenues of realizing a return on an investment when purchasing tax liens.

The first is through redemption. The delinquent tax bill is paid off and the investor receives the funds plus interest and penalties.

The second avenue is through foreclosing on the property. After the specified period of redemption, the lien holder can then file for a deed on the property and thereby take control of it. They can then sell it or rent it out; either option will net them a return on their investment.

Tax Lien Chart

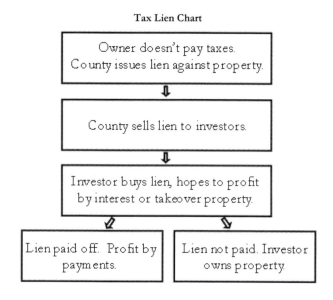

Tax Deeds

A tax deed is a type of legal conveyance similar to a quit claim deed. Unlike tax liens, which simply are debt held against the property, tax deeds give the investor ownership rights to the property in most states.

There are two ways to acquire a tax deed – through a lien conversion in a tax lien state or through a tax deed auction in a tax deed state. A lien conversion means you are converting your tax lien into foreclosure because the redemption period has expired.

For instance, in Arizona, if you purchase a tax lien from the county, and it has not been paid back in three years, you can file for foreclosure and own the property free and clear.

Some states simply sell tax deeds and do not have tax lien auctions; hence, there are no redemption periods or any tax lien conversions to keep track of. You simply own the property immediately after the sale is complete.

Tax deed auctions are typically more expensive than tax lien auctions. The price of tax liens are based off how much property taxes are owed, while the price of tax deeds are usually based on the number of bidders and their perceived market value of that property. Here's an example of a tax deed property for sale in Lee County, FL and what the opening bid was for this piece of land:

12/07/1999		
TD #: <u>1999505958</u>	Legal Description: 100 FT FPL EASMENT SEC 19 PER OR 475 PG 32 OR 0220 PG 0210	
STRAP: 19452700000000010		OPENING BID: $21,821.43
OWNER: WEST COAST TURNAROUND INC		

The opening bid started at $21,821.43. If this was a tax lien sale, the opening bid would have been around $1000.00 rather than $21,821.43.

If for some reason the property doesn't sell at the tax deed auction, it reverts back to the county and the county can upon its own discretion sell it in an over the counter (OTC) sale. This leaves investors with the opportunity to make a purchase of a tax deed without having to bid for it.

Another important thing to keep in mind when considering making an investment at a tax deed sale is that with this type of purchase, the investor is not receiving a warranty deed as you would get with the purchase of a property through conventional means.

Instead, the investor receives either a constable's deed, a bargain and sale deed, or a sheriff's deed. These deeds come with no warranty and are sold "as is".

"As Is" Conveyance

The problem with "as is" property is its resale value. You will not be able to sell it at its full market value without court action or convincing a title company to issue title insurance on it.

Most buyers want to make sure that the property they are buying is without risk; hence, they are reluctant to purchase property that has no warranties. By filing a quiet title suit in court, you will forever remove any doubts about the property's ownership. The cost of quiet title suits depends in court and attorney fees in your area. In South Florida, it costs roughly $3,000-$4,000 per parcel.

You can also seek out title companies that will insure tax deeds. Companies like Tax Title Services offers title insurance for tax deeds sold in Alabama, Georgia, Maryland, South Carolina, California, Illinois, Michigan, Colorado, Indiana, Mississippi, West Virginia, Florida, Louisiana, Missouri, Oklahoma, Tennessee, and New York. Their web site is accessible at www.TaxTitleServices.com.

Their base fees start at $750.00 which is a significantly lower cost than a quiet title suit.

Is This For Me?

Purchasing tax liens and tax deeds at auction offers an investor a better return on investment than many other "safe" investments.

Now that you understand what tax liens and tax deeds are and the difference between the two, how do you know if this type of investing is right for you?

Ask yourself the following questions:

(1) Are you annoyed that you have little or no control with your investment portfolio?
(2) Do you have to guess market trends and read over SEC filings just to achieve 12 percent returns?
(3) Are you finding your investments go up and down dependent on what a supposed Wall Street analyst says on CNBC?

If your answer was "yes" to all of the above questions, then this investment vehicle is definitely right for you. Because it is an "auction format", you control how much you spend and what your risks are. No stock brokers, no middle man.

Day 1 Summary

- Tax liens are like an IOU ("I owe you") certificate for delinquent property taxes. The local government sells the IOU certificate to investors who in turn will get a return when the owner pays back the taxes with interest and penalties.
- If the owner does NOT pay the taxes, he could lose his property to the investor. Even if a mortgage company has a mortgage lien on the property, a tax lien supersedes it and the property will be transferred free and clear.
- Some states do not have tax liens but have tax deeds. Tax deeds convey property rights to the investor.
- Many assume parcels sold at these auctions are dumps – but in reality, they are often valuable properties that have a high resale value.

"Unless you're willing to have a go, fail miserably, and have another go, success won't happen."

-Phillip Adams

Day 2: Before You Start...

It takes money to make money! If you have bags of pocket money stashed away, then skip today's lesson. But for the rest who needs some startup money before starting on this venture, read on.

Investing in new ventures is like starting your own business. You need cash flow and you prefer to have someone else's money to play with rather than your own (ie: the bank's). If you can borrow $1,000 and you make $2,000 out of it – why not do it?

Credit Rating

In most cases, borrowing money requires a good credit rating. If you don't know what your credit rating is, you need to find out today!

As of September 1, 2005, thanks to President Bush and Congress' passing of the Fair and Accurate Credit Transactions Act, you are entitled to a FREE credit report from the three credit bureaus (Equifax, Experian, TransUnion) through one centralized source.

There are many offers of free credit reports on the Internet, but only one web site is facilitated by the government. Please try to avoid sites that tout free services, as they often have additional charges after a free trial of monitoring your credit.

To request your free credit, you can do so online, by phone, or by mail. Here is the contact information:

Toll-free: 1–877–322–8228
Toll-free (TDD): 1–877–730–4104
Web: https://www.annualcreditreport.com/
Annual Credit Report Request Service
PO Box 105283
Atlanta, GA 30348-5283

If you are ordering by the Web, the web site will look similar to this:

You want to make sure you read each credit report carefully and dispute any inaccurate debts or correct any delinquent accounts before applying for any financing from an institution.

You may also want to purchase your credit scores (sometimes called the FICO score), which is a summary of your credit history. The score is calculated and weighed by your payment punctuality (35% weight), ratio of debt to available credit (30% weight), length of credit history (15% weight), types of credit used (10% weight), and how many times you've applied for credit in the past few months (10% weight).

Your credit score could vary anywhere from 300 to 850.

A score of 660 is considered a breaking point for credit worthiness and a score of 720+ is considered above average (you get approved for almost any loans).

Financing by Friends & Family

Friends and family is the first round of financing for any startup investor. There usually no hassles, no credit checks, and no collaterals.

Even the biggest investors of real estate started out this way. For example, Donald Trump, had his father co-sign business loans when he was starting out and gave him seed money for his company.

When Larry Page and Sergey Bin were starting Google, they couldn't convince Yahoo! or other investors to give them money, so they sought out friends and family. Their first big break was for $100,000 from an acquaintance at Sun Microsystems.

Financing by Prosper.com

If you don't want to ask acquaintances, friends, and/or family for money, you can ask strangers online for help – securely!

Using sites like Prosper.com, you can borrow up to $25,000 without any collateral! All you need is a driver's license, a bank account, and a social security number.

Touted as the "eBay equivalent" for personal loans, you can post how much you need (up to $25,000) and what interest rates you are willing to pay for.

Lenders composed of individuals with extra cash will then bid for your loan by a minimum of $50.00 increments.

Example of lenders bidding on a Prosper.com loan:

Bid History			Legend: ✓ = Winning ✓ = Partially winning ✗ = Outbid			? Help
Bidder	Rate	Amount Bid	Winning	Status ▲	Bid Date (PT)	
1stPlace	17.00%	$50.00	$50.00	✓	Aug-26-2006 1:13 AM	
Chewylender	17.00%	$100.00	$100.00	✓	Aug-26-2006 12:18 AM	
boxman	17.00%	$50.00	$50.00	✓	Aug-25-2006 11:53 PM	
crediteur	17.00%	$50.00	$50.00	✓	Aug-25-2006 11:52 PM	
Loan-from-Scott	17.00%	$100.00	$100.00	✓	Aug-25-2006 11:22 PM	
cwndn	17.00%	$100.00	$100.00	✓	Aug-25-2006 11:14 PM	
HawaiiBoy75	17.00%	$100.00	$100.00	✓	Aug-25-2006 11:06 PM	
mpmsfca	17.00%	$95.00	$95.00	✓	Aug-25-2006 10:57 PM	
PMAFunds	17.00%	$50.00	$50.00	✓	Aug-25-2006 10:45 PM	
P2P_Financial	17.00%	$75.00	$75.00	✓	Aug-25-2006 10:44 PM	
puzzleglue	17.00%	$50.00	$50.00	✓	Aug-25-2006 10:40 PM	
MartyTwice	17.00%	$50.00	$50.00	✓	Aug-25-2006 10:10 PM	

Once your loan request is bid on by other lenders and is completed, a monthly payment schedule will be arranged by Prosper and your money can be automatically deposited to your bank account.

Financing by Angel Investors

Angel investors are fairly affluent folks that have already done their rounds in business. They have money and are willing to spend it for the right causes and if you have the right sales pitch.

Inc.com has a great resource online about angel investors. You can access articles about getting financing from angels through here:

http://www.inc.com/guides/start_biz/24011.html

Financing by Banks - Lines of Credit

Several institutions have "lines of credit" programs for small businesses and investors. A line of credit allows you to borrow money an infinite amount of times without reapplying as long as it doesn't exceed the credit limit allocated for your account. It's much like a credit card but without the 24% interest rates.

After the bank sets your credit limit, you'll be given a checkbook and/or a VISA/MasterCard card to use for your spending. Lines of credit interest rates hover around 7-8% which is far better than most credit cards.

Here are some banks/institutions that can offer a line of credit without needing any collateral for your business:

Bank of America
Program: Business Credit Express (up to $100,000)
Phone: 1-888-600-4000
Web: http://www.bankofamerica.com/small_business

Capital One
Program: Business Line of Credit (up to $50,000)
Phone: 1-800-205-2282
Web: http://www.capitalone.com/smallbusiness/

Financing by IRA and Retirement Account

A little-known IRS provision lets you extend your real estate purchasing with tax-deferred dollars.

BY KELLI L. CLICK

Are stock market woes preventing you from building wealth in your retirement account? If so, you might be interested in a small, but growing, trend among individual retirement account owners—investing their retirement funds in real estate.

How It Works

If the option of using tax-deferred funds to purchase property sounds appealing, you'll need to locate an independent IRA custodian that allows real estate investments and work with that company to set up an IRA account. Most banks and brokerage companies—the most common IRA account options—limit your choices to certificates of deposit, stocks, mutual funds, annuities, and similar financial instruments. But Section 408 of the Internal Revenue Code permits individuals to purchase land, commercial property, condominiums, residential property, trust deeds, or real estate contracts with funds held in many common forms of IRAs, including a traditional IRA, a Roth IRA, and a Simplified Employee Pension plan, or SEP-IRA.

To find a custodian that specializes in real estate, search under terms such as "real estate IRA" or "self-directed IRA." This latter term was coined by the financial industry in the 1980s to distinguish the self-directed IRA from other IRAs that focus on stocks and bonds. The IRA account holder can't serve as the custodian of his or her own account. However, it's important to select a custodian knowledgeable about the types of investment you're interested in, because the custodian holds title to the real estate. Do your homework, and understand what you're getting into.

Fees can vary widely among custodians, as can the flexibility of the services provided for account holders. If the custodian holds real estate on your behalf, but does not service it (collect the rent, etc.), you may have to contract with other providers. However, be sure that all rents are paid into the IRA and that all taxes are paid by the IRA.

Purchasing the Property

Most IRA custodians that hold real estate will usually allow you to purchase raw or vacant land, residential properties, or commercial buildings for your portfolio. In addition, most custodians do not permit foreign property. However, many custodians now allow leveraged property.

Since buying a property may require more funds than you currently have available in your IRA, you also can have your IRA purchase an interest in the property in conjunction with other individuals, such as a spouse, business associate, or friend. Also keep in mind that if the property is leveraged, the debt must be a non-recourse promissory note.

Unfortunately, Internal Revenue Service regulations will not let you use the real estate owned by your IRA as your residence or vacation home. Nor can your business lease space in your IRA-held property. The underlying premise for any real estate investment purchased with IRA funds is that you can't have any personal use or benefit of the property. To do so may cost you plenty in taxes and penalties.

There are a few other IRS limitations as well. You cannot place a real estate property that you already own into your IRA. Your spouse, your parents, or your children also couldn't have owned the property before it was purchased by your IRA. Property owned by siblings may be allowed, since the Internal Revenue Code (section 4975) specifies that only "lineal descendents" be disqualified.

Once you've chosen a property, your IRA custodian—not you personally—must actually purchase it. The title will reflect the name of your IRA custodian for your benefit (such as Silver Trust Co., Custodian FBO John Doe IRA). In addition, you'll need to direct your IRA custodian to pay the earnest money from your IRA account.

Operating an IRA-held Property

Because all property expenses, including taxes, insurance, and repairs, must be paid from funds in your IRA, you'll need liquid funds available in your account. Of course, all income generated from the property will be deposited in your IRA account so you can use that money to cover your costs. You also can make annual contributions within federal guidelines.

For tax years 2006-2007, you can contribute $4,000 ($5,000 for 2008) annually to a traditional or Roth IRA ($4,500 if you're age 50 or older) and as much as 25 percent of your annual compensation, up to $44,000, if you're a self-employed individual with a SEP-IRA. If your account doesn't have funds to cover property expenses, you will have to withdraw the property from your IRA and pay taxes on the value of the property, as well as possible penalties for early withdrawal.

It's also possible to sell properties while they are held by your IRA, so long as the purchaser is not a family member. Once a deal closes, your IRA account holds the cash proceeds—ready for you to make your next investment. An alternative is to sell an IRA-held property with seller financing so that all payments made by the buyers are paid to the IRA.

Distributing Your Property

You can withdraw real estate from your IRA and use it as a residence or second home when you reach retirement age (age 59½ or older for a penalty-free withdrawal). At that time, you can elect either to have the IRA sell the property or take an in-kind distribution of the property. Under that arrangement, your IRA custodian assigns the title to the property to you. You will then have to pay income taxes on the current value of the property if it's been held in a traditional IRA. If the property was held in a Roth IRA, you won't owe taxes at distribution. This makes a Roth IRA extremely attractive if you anticipate that your real estate investments will appreciate over time.

Whether your retirement strategy is to hold properties or buy and sell for gain, real estate investing through your IRA can yield extraordinary returns toward your future retirement.

IRA Options

While any form of IRA allows for real estate investment, there are other pluses and minuses to consider when choosing the account type that's best for you:
- A **traditional IRA** lets you deduct annual contributions (which for 2006 increases to $4,000, or $4,500 if you're age 50 or older) from your income. However, once you begin withdrawing money, those funds will be taxed as regular income.
- A **Roth IRA** gives you no deduction on your current contributions (again $4,000), but does allow you to withdraw funds tax-free. If you expect to buy a real estate investment in an IRA and hold it for a long period, this is

probably your best option, particularly if the property increases in value over that period.

- A **SEP-IRA** is designed for self-employed individuals and small companies. You can contribute up to 25 percent of your compensation, or $44,000, whichever is less. However, keep in mind that if you have employees, you must make contributions for them as well. This option is a great alternative for real estate practitioners who can make the higher contributions because they can build up funds more rapidly to purchase properties. Withdrawals from a SEP-IRA are treated like those of a traditional IRA for tax purposes.

*Kelli L. Click is vice president of sales and marketing at Sterling Trust Co., a self-directed IRA and 401(k) custodian, in Waco, Texas. She can be reached at 800/955-3434, ext.**5077.***

Investing As A Corporate Entity

You need to decide whether you want to invest as an individual or as a corporate entity for liability reasons. Especially in tax deed auctions.

Owners and partners of a corporation or LLC have a certain level of protection against their personal assets. When someone is injured on your investment property, you are personally liable for the victim's loss of income and medical costs. You can "shift" that responsibility if the property is owned by a corporate entity.

Consider one extreme case in New York. A thief was able to sue the property owner because he was injured when he was trying to rob the store. Employees beat him with a metal pipe as he was trying to intimidate people with a semiautomatic pistol. Luckily, the individual owners of the store were protected through the "corporation"; hence, their personal assets were not in danger.

Though it is unlikely that you'll be sued for injuries sustained in your investment property, it is nonetheless prudent; in making sure you minimize your personal risk by having liability protection through a corporate entity.

You can learn about different corporate types and how to register with your state by contacting Nolo.com at http://www.nolo.com/. Their phone number is (800) 728-3555. Their mailing address is: 950 Parker Street, Berkeley CA 94710-2524.

Insurance

As an entrepreneur, risks are part of the game, but it doesn't necessarily have to hurt you.

Having business insurance to cover your real estate investments gives you a peace of mind, knowing that you are protected even if something goes wrong.

Most investors consider business insurance as an expense instead of an investment. You see, it doesn't matter if you acquired $1 million dollars in assets if you're only to lose it to a lawsuit.

There are three main types of business insurance: liability, people, and property.

Liability insurance covers your business if it conducted actions (or lack of) that resulted in damages. For instance, the normal slip and fall lawsuit falls under this category.

People insurance covers employees, and most of it is optional. Health, dental, and vision insurance falls into this category. As a sole investor in your real estate auctions, you won't need this in the beginning.

Property is what you need to cover your buildings (leased or owned), rental properties, vehicles, equipment, and even intangible properties like trademarks from mishaps, fire, or other types of loss.

You can get more information about these insurance types and how much it cost for you by contacting one of the following firms:

Techinsurance
http://www.techinsurance.com
1301 Central Expy South Suite 115

Allen, TX 75013
(800) 668-7020

NetQuote
http://www.netquote.com
860 Blake Street, Suite 900
Denver, CO 80202
(800) 795.2886

Bank Accounts

You want to place your investment funds in a separate bank account from your normal checking accounts or personal savings accounts.

By keeping it separate, you're making it a lot easier to track your investment money and how it's performing. Check out the local banks in your area, or you could use the following online banks for an easy checking account that you can setup online:

Citibank – 1-800-374-9500
http://www.citibank.com
100 Citibank Drive
P.O. Box 769004
San Antonio, TX 78245-9004
Products: Offers a variety of products as well as 5% checking (Rate as of Sept 2006).

Netbank.com - 1-888-256-6932
http://www.netbank.com
1015 Windward Ridge Parkway
Alpharetta, GA 30005
Products: Offer interest business checking and online banking.

Finance Software

You don't have to spend a pretty penny to get financial software. There are a couple of easy-to-use, affordable financial software solutions for investors.

You'll be able to track your income sources, expenses (ie: road trips to tax auctions) with ease using either Microsoft Money or Quicken. It can also print out budget reports, and even help you with your taxes.

$29.99 on Amazon.com
Microsoft Money 2007 Deluxe

$44.95 on Amazon.com
Quicken Deluxe 2007 by Intuit

Tracking Software

If you'll be investing in tax liens heavily, you'll need to be able to track what date you purchased your tax lien, its redemption period, interest rates, if and when it was redeemed, and your profit/loss. Additionally, if you're driving to tax auctions, your mileage is tax deductible!

You'll want to use Microsoft Excel for this task or you can download the free OpenOffice suite alternative.

Both software programs allow you to add the aggregate numbers in fields and columns, giving you an easy way to calculate your gross costs or return.

You can also use Excel or OpenOffice to keep track of your tax deeds – when you purchased them, when you sold them, and your costs/expenses.

Your accountant will thank you at the end of the year for being able to keep track of your investments so neatly. Also, if you need assistance on how to track your tax liens/tax deeds on Excel, you can download templates from the book's web site at http://www.InvestingWithoutLosing.com.

Microsoft Excel
Available on Amazon.com, BestBuy or other retailers.
BestBuy: 800-276-5107
Est retail price: $189.00

OpenOffice
http://www.openoffice.org/
Est retail price: FREE

Make sure you talk to your accountant on how to format your
tracking methods in Excel.

As much as possible, you want to imitate the necessary fields
required in your tax returns such as when a property was acquired,
when it was sold, the original cost, and other pertinent information.

Pictures!

Buying a digital camera can be quite helpful when you are doing
property research (see day 4). Before the auction begins, you can
start taking pictures of the property that potentially interests you.
Good digital cameras, like Kodak's EasyShare, can run as cheap as
$69.00 on Amazon.com and other retail stores. Additionally, most
new cell phones come with 1.2+ megapixels and can actually serve
the same purpose.

Some suggestions on what to do with your camera:
1. Take a picture of the property.
2. Take a picture of the neighborhood.
3. Take a picture of the views -- north, east, west, south.

If you are buying tax deeds for a quick flip, taking pictures is an
absolute must. You can sell property faster with pictures in your
listings.

Bena, Minnesota
(City lot purchased for $250.00)

Delaware County, Indiana
(Tax deed property for sale by American Tax Funding - $10,000)

St. Louis County, Minnesota
(Tax deed commercial property - $3,000)

Day 2 Summary

- You can acquire seed money from friends and family, angel investors, or even strangers through online sites like Prosper.com.
- Investing as a corporation or LLC protects your personal assets.
- Business insurance gives another level of protection by offsetting the costs of litigation.
- Having a separate bank account for your investment funds allow for easier accounting.
- Using a finance software like Microsoft Money or Intuit's Quicken gives you better control of your income and expenses.
- Use Microsoft Excel or the free OpenOffice to track your tax liens and tax deeds easily. You can download free templates on how to track tax liens/deeds by accessing www.InvestingWithoutLosing.com.
- Get a digital camera for taking pictures, or use your cell phone camera – this is especially necessary for tax deed sales requiring a quick flip.

"Many of life's failures are people who did not realize how close they were to success when they gave up."

-Thomas Alva Edison

Day 3: Where To Find Tax Auctions

D oes your state offer tax lien auctions? Do they have tax deed auctions? Do they offer both? Today, you'll discover which type of auction is offered in your state and what to expect at the auction.

It's highly recommended that you start out investing in tax liens and/or tax deeds locally. You don't have to travel far and you know the area.

In most home towns, there are places that you shouldn't go to alone and there are places that you can freely travel without any problems. You know where the upscale properties are located and you know where the lower valued areas are at; hence, it should be easy for you to realize whether something is worth its bid price when you're participating in an auction.

What Type of Tax Sale Does Your State Offer?

In the previous day, you learned that counties and parishes collect real estate taxes from the property owners. If they do not pay it, the county will balance their budget by selling liens.

The type of public auctions held depends on the state in which the property is located. About half of the states offer tax lien sales, the other half offer tax deed sales only, and some offer both.

Auctions in each state usually have the following type of bidding formats (more on this on day five):

1. "Bid down" interest bidding: States like Florida and Arizona bid down the interest rates of the tax lien certificate. To win, your bid must be the lowest interest rate.
2. "Premium" bidding: States like Colorado and Alabama bid over the value of the lien. To win, you must have the highest bid (ie: Instead of a $100.00 value on a lien, you bid $150.00 to win it).
3. Over the counter (OTC): Over the counter sales (OTC) are parcels sold without going through a public auction. This is extremely convenient for investors that do not have the time or the capability to travel to different counties or states. Most over the counter parcels can be purchased on the phone, online, or by mail!
4. Random bidding: County auctioneer selects a bidder randomly to see if he would like to bid on the property, if not, he moves to the next random bidder.
5. Rotational bidding: County auctioneer gives each bidder the ability to purchase equal amount of tax liens.
6. Sealed envelope bidding: Your bid is sealed on an envelope and the highest bid wins. Sometimes this is done by mail rather than in an auction house setting.

All of these terms, rules and regulations can be confusing to a new investor. It makes it even more confusing if you aren't sure what your state offers in the way of tax deed or tax lien; hence, the chart below was created to guide you on what options are available in your state.

State	Type	Bid Type	Over the Counter	Interest Rates	Period of Redemption
Alabama	Lien	Premium/Yes		12% annum	3 years
Alaska	Deed	Varies/Yes		N/A	1 year
Arizona	Lien	Bid Down/Yes		16% annum	3-5 years
Arkansas	Deed	Premium/No		N/A	30 days
California	Deed	Premium/No		N/A	N/A

Colorado	Lien	Premium/Varies	Varies	3 years
Connecticut	Deed Hybrid	Premium/No	18% annum	1 year
Delaware	Deed Hybrid	Premium/No	15% penalty	60 days
Florida	Lien	Bid Down/No Liens but Deeds Sold	18% down to 5% min.	2 years
Georgia	Deed Hybrid	Premium/No	20% penalty	1 year
Hawaii	Deed Hybrid	Premium/No	12% annum	1 year
Idaho	Deed	Premium/No	N/A	N/A
Illinois	Lien	Bid Down/No	18% penalty	2-3 years
Indiana	Lien	Premium/No	10-15% penalty	1 year
Iowa	Lien	Rotates/No	24% annum	2 years
Kansas	Deed	Premium/No	N/A	N/A
Kentucky	Lien	Premium/No	12% annum	1 year
Louisiana	Deed Hybrid	Bid Down/No	12% annum + 5% penalty	3 years
Maine	Deed	Sealed/No	N/A	N/A
Maryland	Lien	Premium/Yes	6-24% annum	6 months
Massachusetts	Deed Hybrid	Premium/No	16% annum	6 months
Michigan	Deed	Premium/No	N/A	N/A
Minnesota	Deed	Premium/Yes	N/A	N/A
Mississippi	Lien	Premium/Yes	18% annum on lien	2 years
Missouri	Lien	Premium/No	10% annum + 8% on further taxes	2 years
Montana	Lien	Rotates/Yes	10% annum + 2% penalty	3 years

Nebraska	Lien	Rotates/Yes	14% annum	3 years
Nevada	Deed	Premium/No	N/A	N/A
New Hampshire	Deed	Premium/No	N/A	N/A
New Jersey	Lien	Bid Down on Premium/No	18% annum	2 years
New Mexico	Deed	Premium/No	N/A	N/A
New York	Deed	Premium/No	N/A	N/A
North Carolina	Deed	Premium/No	N/A	N/A
North Dakota	Lien	Premium/No	12% annum	3 years
Ohio	Deed and Lien	Premium/No	18% annum for lien	3 years for lien
Oklahoma	Lien	Rotates/Yes	8%	2 years
Oregon	Deed	Premium/Varies	N/A	N/A
Pennsylvania	Deed Hybrid/ Varies by property	Premium/Varies	10% when applicable	1 year when applicable
Rhode Island	Deed Hybrid	Premium/No	10% penalty + 1% penalty a month starting with 7th month	1 year
South Carolina	Lien	Premium/Yes	8-12% annum	1 year
South Dakota	Lien	Premium/Yes	12% annum	3 years
Tennessee	Deed Hybrid	Premium/No	10% annum	1 year
Texas	Deed Hybrid	Premium/Varies	25% penalty	6 months – 2 years
Utah	Deed	Premium/No	N/A	N/A
Vermont	Lien	Varies by Town/Varies by Town	12% annum	1 year
Virginia	Deed	Premium/No	N/A	N/A
Washington	Deed	Premium/No	N/A	N/A

West Virginia	Lien	Premium/No Liens but Deeds Sold	12% annum	17 months
Wisconsin	Deed	Premium & Sealed/No	N/A	N/A
Wyoming	Lien	Rotates/Yes	15% annum + 3% penalty	4 years

As a rule of thumb, you should always check with your local county officials regarding the rules and regulations of auctions in your area. Laws could change, and this chart could be outdated.

You probably noticed on the list that some states have "N/A" in place of interest rates and redemption periods. This is because those states are "pure" tax deed states. These states overwhelmingly sell only tax deeds.

Please note Alaska has a circumstance unlike any of the other states. This state does not offer tax lien or tax deed sales. After a one year redemption period, the taxing municipalities, which take ownership of the property at the time taxes are delinquent, will sell the property at fair market value to the public.

Alaska's Department of Natural Resources also sells parcels separately from local jurisdictions through over the counter sales.

Tax Deed States That Can 'Legally' Have Tax Lien Sales

The following is a list of tax deed states that can legally have tax lien sales. They have it on the books by state statutes but often times they do not exercise it. If you have questions about tax lien sales in these particular states, contact the local county assessor or county treasurer.

> ➤ Arkansas
> ➤ California
> ➤ Massachusetts
> ➤ Michigan
> ➤ Nevada
> ➤ New Hampshire
> ➤ New York

> Ohio
> Wisconsin

Where Do I Find a Tax Lien or Tax Deed?

Typically, tax lien states host their auctions annually while tax deed states conduct sales more often. For instance, Texas, a hybrid state, hosts monthly sales while California, a tax deed state offers biannual sales.

The duration between sales, amount of days per sale, and number of liens or deeds up for sale will vary depending on population of municipality and local government preference.

Investors can find information about local upcoming sales by watching for announcements in their local newspapers. Legal notices are usually announced with large bold headers and it will state that there is a public auction or tax lien sales about to take place. Advertisements are usually posted two weeks to four weeks before the sale.

If you want to find out about public auctions outside of your local jurisdiction, the best tool to use is the Internet! Although publications and paper references are outdated the moment they are printed, the Internet is usually up to date. Additionally, you can access this book's web site (www.InvestingWithoutLosing.com) for more information on upcoming tax auctions.

Tax Auctions Held Online

Some counties have also taken the next step to public tax auctions. They've put them online! Here are some counties that have put their tax auction online:
- AZ: Yuma County
  o (http://www.co.yuma.az.us/treas/)
- CO: Jefferson County
  o (http://www.co.jefferson.co.us/treasurer/treasurer_T68_R9.htm)

- FL: Leon County
  - (http://www.clerk.leon.fl.us/index.php?section=1&server=&page=clerk_services/finance/tax_deeds.html)
- FL: Orange County
  - (http://www.BidOrangeCounty.com)

What To Expect At An Auction

Live auctions are fun and exciting. But before you can jump into the middle of the action, you need to know what to expect. Before any auction starts, there are a few things that need to happen:

1. The county will need to provide a list of tax liens or tax deeds that's up for sale. This is often times published in a newspaper, posted on the Internet, and/or available at the local tax collector/treasurer's office.
2. You will need to fill out an IRS W-9 form for tax lien sales. This is used to report to the IRS for any interest payments you or your business may receive.
3. You may need to fill out a bidder application form.

Tax Deed and Tax Lien Lists

The property list for tax lien or tax deed sales are usually available three to four weeks in advance of the sale. This gives you an ample amount of time to review and research what's for sale.

Most tax lien and tax deed property lists come with a parcel number, legal description, and the total tax due (or for tax deeds, the minimum bid amount to purchase).

The parcel number is the main number you use to lookup property information online or through the county assessor/appraiser. You'll learn more about researching properties on day four. For now, concentrate on how the auction process works and try to recognize the formats of different tax lien/tax deed lists.

Here's an example of a tax lien list published by Coconino County, Arizona:

Delinquent Tax Lien List as of June 1, 2006

Item	Book	Map	Parcel	Legal Description	Total Due
1	100	00	003	100 43 003A 216 W PHOENIX AVE	$7,090.04
60	107	10	001Z	ALL THOSE PORS SW4SE4 & SE4SW4 SEC 14 21N-7E LYNG S OF SF R*	$3,570.85
64	107	25	002A	ELK RUN POR *	$100.15
71	108	10	085B	GREENLAW ESTATES NO 3. NO 1' LOT 27. *	$1,185.49
83	110	00	702	110 08 702U USGS GOVT BLDG NO 3	$14,314.90
98	112	00	002	OUT OF PARCEL 112-01-700 ON S*	$46,752.43
141	115	07	273	MOUNTAINAIRE UNIT 1 POR OF SAGINAW-MANISTEE RR R/W LYNGTO L*	$622.75
432	203	52	004	E 30' W2NW4SE4 SEC 14 22N-4E. EXCEPT:NLY 50' THEREOF. *	$187.17
442	205	08	010	KAIBAB KNOLLS EST #13 LOT 722 *	$2,210.96
448	205	08	040	KAIBAB KNOLLS EST #13 LOT 768 *	$1,318.61
454	205	09	040	KAIBAB KNOLLS EST #13A LOT 7016 *	$2,210.96
455	205	09	063	KAIBAB KNOLLS EST #13A LOT 7039 *	$1,803.51
492	206	02	008	KAIBAB KNOLLS EST #7 LOT 337 *	$3,281.59
493	206	03	003	KAIBAB KNOLLS EST #7 LOT 323 *	$1,846.05
494	206	03	033	KAIBAB KNOLLS EST #7 LOT 381 *	$954.17
498	206	05	001	KAIBAB KNOLLS EST #7 LOT 193 *	$1,235.06
503	206	07	003	KAIBAB KNOLLS EST #8 LOT 67 *	$1,846.05
505	206	07	014	KAIBAB KNOLLS EST #8 LOT 94 *	$1,846.05
509	206	07	041	KAIBAB KNOLLS EST #8 LOT 153 *	$1,669.28
601	206	54	026	KAIBAB KNOLLS EST #19 LOT 939 *	$1,669.28
602	206	54	033	KAIBAB KNOLLS EST #19 LOT 946 *	$1,182.23

Here's an example of a tax deed list published by Navajo County, Arizona:

Prospective purchasers are advised that: 1) ALL SALES ARE FINAL; 2) THE TITLE CONVEYED BY TREASURER'S DEED MAY OR MAY NOT BE MARKETABLE; 3) EXAMINE PROPERTY BEFORE PURCHASING; 4) CHECK THE ASSESSOR'S MAP FOR THE LOCATION OF THE PARCEL; 5) SEEK ADVICE ON MARKETABILITY OF TITLE CONVEYED BY A TREASURER'S DEED; 6) NO WARRANTIES OR GUARANTEES AS TO THE SIZE OR CONDITION OF PROPERTY AND; 7) NO REFUNDS WILL BE MADE.

Kathy Hieb, Deputy Clerk Of The Board Of Supervisors

PARCEL #	YR	LEGAL DESCRIPTION	DUE
105-09-198C	04	AZ Ranchero #13 Lot 68 less RR R/W	412
105-09-133A	04	AZ RANCHERO, RANCHO #12 LOTS 85 & 112, LESS RR R/W OUT OF 105-09-133	881
105-09-133B	04	AZ RANCHERO, RANCHO #12 LOTS 67 & 84 LESS RR R/W OUT OF 105-09-133	980
105-27-088A	04	AZ RANCHERO, RANCHO #35 LOT 33	4612
105-28-020	92	VEIN OF GOLD 12 Lt 20	334
105-28-021	98	VEIN OF GOLD #12 Lt 21	352
105-28-022	98	VEIN OF GOLD #12 Lt 22	352
105-28-023	98	VEIN OF GOLD #12 Lt 23	352
105-28-033	86	VEIN OF GOLD 12 Lt 33	334
105-28-034	86	VEIN OF GOLD 12 Lt 34	334
105-28-035	86	VEIN OF GOLD 12 Lt 35	334
105-28-036	86	VEIN OF GOLD 12 Lt 36	334
105-28-037	86	VEIN OF GOLD 12 Lt 37	334
105-28-038	86	VEIN OF GOLD 12 Lt 38	334
105-28-039	86	VEIN OF GOLD 12 Lt 39	334
105-28-040	86	VEIN OF GOLD 12 Lt 40	334
105-28-041	86	VEIN OF GOLD 12 Lt 41	334
105-28-042	86	VEIN OF GOLD 12 Lt 42	334
105-28-043	86	VEIN OF GOLD 12 Lt 43	334
105-28-044	86	VEIN OF GOLD 12 Lt 44	334
105-28-053	86	VEIN OF GOLD 12 Lt 53	334
105-28-054	86	VEIN OF GOLD 12 Lt 54	334
105-28-055	86	VEIN OF GOLD 12 Lt 55	334
105-28-056	86	VEIN OF GOLD 12 Lt 56	334
105-28-057	86	VEIN OF GOLD 12 Lt 57	334
105-28-058	86	VEIN OF GOLD 12 Lt 58	334
105-28-059	86	VEIN OF GOLD 12 Lt 59	334
105-28-060	86	VEIN OF GOLD 12 Lt 60	334
105-28-061	86	VEIN OF GOLD 12 Lt 61	334
105-28-062	86	VEIN OF GOLD 12 Lt 62	334
105-28-063	86	VEIN OF GOLD 12 Lt 63	334
105-28-064	03	VEIN OF GOLD 12 Lt 64	445
105-28-070	86	VEIN OF GOLD 12 Lt 70	334
105-28-071	86	VEIN OF GOLD 12 Lt 71	334
105-28-072	86	VEIN OF GOLD 12 Lt 72	334
105-28-073	86	VEIN OF GOLD 12 Lt 73	334
105-28-074	86	VEIN OF GOLD 12 Lt 74	334
105-28-075	86	VEIN OF GOLD 12 Lt 75	334
105-28-076	86	VEIN OF GOLD 12 Lt 76	334
105-28-077	86	VEIN OF GOLD 12 Lt 77	334
105-28-116	86	VEIN OF GOLD 12 Lt 116	334
105-28-141	91	VEIN OF GOLD 12 Lt 141	369
105-28-142	91	VEIN OF GOLD 12 Lt 142	369
105-28-143	91	VEIN OF GOLD 12 Lt 143	369
105-28-144	91	VEIN OF GOLD 12 Lt 144	369
105-28-145	91	VEIN OF GOLD 12 Lt 145	369
105-28-146	91	VEIN OF GOLD 12 Lt 146	369
105-28-147	91	VEIN OF GOLD 12 Lt 147	369
105-28-148	91	VEIN OF GOLD 12 Lt 148	369
105-28-151	91	VEIN OF GOLD 12 Lt 151	369
105-28-152	91	VEIN OF GOLD 12 Lt 152	369
105-28-153	91	VEIN OF GOLD 12 Lt 153	369
105-28-154	91	VEIN OF GOLD 12 Lt 154	369
105-28-155	91	VEIN OF GOLD 12 Lt 155	369
105-28-156	91	VEIN OF GOLD 12 Lt 156	369
105-28-157	91	VEIN OF GOLD 12 Lt 157	369
105-28-158	91	VEIN OF GOLD 12 Lt 158	369

In both of these lists, the parcel number is used as the primary method of identifying the property. You'll learn in day four on how to use the parcel number to help you judge whether a property is worth investing in.

What To Expect At An Auction: IRS W-9 Form

In tax lien auctions, Form W-9 is required for all investors to fill out. The county may provide this during the sale or before the sale.

On the W-9 form, you will be required to report your Social Security number or your tax id if you are bidding as a business entity.

The county needs your W-9 form to report interest payments (if any) to the IRS. The W-9 form is relatively easy to fill out and is only one page long. You'll need to input your name, address, social security number or tax id, phone number, and signature. A sample of what the form looks like is available on the next page.

You can also download the W-9 form directly from the IRS' web site or you can contact them by phone. The information for the IRS is as follows:

Internal Revenue Service
401 W. Peachtree St. NW
Atlanta, GA 30308
http://www.irs.gov
1-800-829-1040

Typical W-9 form

Form W-9 (Rev. November 2005) Department of the Treasury Internal Revenue Service	**Request for Taxpayer Identification Number and Certification**	Give form to the requester. Do not send to the IRS.

Print or type — See Specific Instructions on page 2.

Name (as shown on your income tax return)

Business name, if different from above

Check appropriate box: ☐ Individual/ Sole proprietor ☐ Corporation ☐ Partnership ☐ Other ▶ ....   ☐ Exempt from backup withholding

Address (number, street, and apt. or suite no.)   Requester's name and address (optional)

City, state, and ZIP code

List account number(s) here (optional)

Part I   Taxpayer Identification Number (TIN)

Enter your TIN in the appropriate box. The TIN provided must match the name given on Line 1 to avoid backup withholding. For individuals, this is your social security number (SSN). However, for a resident alien, sole proprietor, or disregarded entity, see the Part I instructions on page 3. For other entities, it is your employer identification number (EIN). If you do not have a number, see How to get a TIN on page 3.

Note. If the account is in more than one name, see the chart on page 4 for guidelines on whose number to enter.

Social security number

or

Employer identification number

Part II   Certification

Under penalties of perjury, I certify that:

1. The number shown on this form is my correct taxpayer identification number (or I am waiting for a number to be issued to me), and

2. I am not subject to backup withholding because: (a) I am exempt from backup withholding, or (b) I have not been notified by the Internal Revenue Service (IRS) that I am subject to backup withholding as a result of a failure to report all interest or dividends, or (c) the IRS has notified me that I am no longer subject to backup withholding, and

3. I am a U.S. person (including a U.S. resident alien).

Certification instructions. You must cross out item 2 above if you have been notified by the IRS that you are currently subject to backup withholding because you have failed to report all interest and dividends on your tax return. For real estate transactions, item 2 does not apply. For mortgage interest paid, acquisition or abandonment of secured property, cancellation of debt, contributions to an individual retirement arrangement (IRA), and generally, payments other than interest and dividends, you are not required to sign the Certification, but you must provide your correct TIN. (See the Instructions on page 4.)

Sign Here   Signature of U.S. person ▶   Date ▶

Purpose of Form

A person who is required to file an information return with the IRS, must obtain your correct taxpayer identification number (TIN) to report, for example, income paid to you, real estate transactions, mortgage interest you paid, acquisition or abandonment of secured property, cancellation of debt, or contributions you made to an IRA.

U.S. person. Use Form W-9 only if you are a U.S. person (including a resident alien), to provide your correct TIN to the person requesting it (the requester) and, when applicable, to:

1. Certify that the TIN you are giving is correct (or you are waiting for a number to be issued),

2. Certify that you are not subject to backup withholding, or

3. Claim exemption from backup withholding if you are a U.S. exempt payee.

In 3 above, if applicable, you are also certifying that as a U.S. person, your allocable share of any partnership income from a U.S. trade or business is not subject to the withholding tax on foreign partners' share of effectively connected income.

Note. If a requester gives you a form other than Form W-9 to request your TIN, you must use the requester's form if it is substantially similar to this Form W-9.

For federal tax purposes, you are considered a person if you are:

● An individual who is a citizen or resident of the United States,

● A partnership, corporation, company, or association created or organized in the United States or under the laws of the United States, or

● Any estate (other than a foreign estate) or trust. See Regulations sections 301.7701-6(a) and 7(a) for additional information.

Special rules for partnerships. Partnerships that conduct a trade or business in the United States are generally required to pay a withholding tax on any foreign partners' share of income from such business. Further, in certain cases where a Form W-9 has not been received, a partnership is required to presume that a partner is a foreign person, and pay the withholding tax. Therefore, if you are a U.S. person that is a partner in a partnership conducting a trade or business in the United States, provide Form W-9 to the partnership to establish your U.S. status and avoid withholding on your share of partnership income.

The person who gives Form W-9 to the partnership for purposes of establishing its U.S. status and avoiding withholding on its allocable share of net income from the partnership conducting a trade or business in the United States is in the following cases:

● The U.S. owner of a disregarded entity and not the entity,

Cat. No. 10231X   Form **W-9** (Rev. 11-2005)

Bidder Application Form

Most counties will use the W-9 form to keep a record of who bid on the auction. Some counties require additional paperwork. The purpose of the bidder application form is to keep track of all the participants in the sale. It also makes it easier for county officials to keep track of the bidder number assignments.

Typical bidder application form
COCONINO COUNTY TREASURER BIDDER INFORMATION CARD
(Please Print)
Bidder Number_____
(Treasurer's office use only)

Bidder's Name/s as it is to appear on the Certificate of Purchase
Address_____ Phone Number:(____)_____

FEDERAL WITHHOLDING INFORMATION
Please enter your taxpayer identification number on the appropriate line:
_____or_____
Social Security Number   Employer Identification
Name of person or entity whose number is listed above:

I affirm the above tax identification number is correct and that I will report
all interest income from my tax liens annually to the U.S. Internal Revenue Service and the Arizona
Department of Revenue.

_____   _____
Signature   Date

Proxy Bidding

In some counties you are allowed to have proxy bidders. These are individuals who bid for you (or your company). Many seasoned investors often times have auctions occurring at the same time and cannot be at two different places at the same time; hence, using proxy bidders allows them to participate in both auctions without missing a beat.

A proxy bidder must be trustworthy, as he will be the one bidding for you. On day five, you'll learn how to conduct bidding strategies with a proxy bidder.

Day 3 Summary

- Each state is either a tax lien state, tax deed state, or a hybrid state.
- Each state has different formats for auction bidding.
- To participate in a real estate auction, you have to fill out basic paperwork: an application form and an IRS form to report monies paid in tax lien sales.
- It is important that you contact the local county authority on how they conduct their public auctions. Use the chart found in today's chapter to get a general idea of how each state works.
- You can access this book's web site as a resource in helping you find tax auctions in your area: http://www.InvestingWithoutLosing.com
- You don't have to leave home to participate in some tax auctions. Some counties have placed their tax sales online!
- It's important to gather information about a tax auction days ahead of time (if not weeks ahead of time). By gathering the property lists and researching parcels, you'll learn which liens or deeds to bid on.
- All interest payments from tax liens are reported to the IRS using either your social security number or tax ID.

Day 4

"If you think you can, you can. And if you think you can't, you're right."

-Henry Ford

Day 4: Research Before The Auction

Yesterday you learned how to look for tax auctions and which particular states have tax deeds or tax lien auctions. Additionally, you learned what paperwork is needed to be filled out before you can participate in the auction.

When you find a tax auction you like, you need to learn how to decipher the information the county gives you such as the property list they publish for the upcoming auction.

Today, you will learn how to research the properties on these lists and conduct your due diligence. You will also learn how to identify risks involved in specific kinds of properties.

Why Do I Have To Research?

Tax liens and tax deeds have unique risks. Today you'll learn how to minimize those risks by researching. The old wise saying of "look before you leap" is our theme for today.

Here are some common risks that you'll face when you invest in tax liens and/or tax deed auctions:

1. Tax liens: It isn't liquid. You obviously have to wait for the property owner to pay the taxes to get a return on your investment or wait out the redemption period to own the property.

   This is one major risk of a tax lien because if you fall on financial hardship, you can't liquidate it easily. There are some jurisdictions that allow you to assign or sell your tax lien to someone else, though there may be additional fees that the county will charge.

2. Tax liens & tax deeds: IRS liens. Some counties, like those in California, will "flag" a property that has an IRS lien on it; hence giving a warning to the investor that there is more risk involved. Some counties won't even put tax liens up for sale if they have IRS liens on them.

   The risk here is an IRS lien cannot be wiped out. The IRS has 120 days from the public sale of any property to execute their right and can buy you out from your lien or deed. If they don't exercise that right after 120 days, the IRS can no longer buy the lien or deed from you.

   If you still seek to buy a property with an IRS lien on it, don't make any improvements on the property until the 120 days passes. The IRS will NOT reimburse you for any improvements if they exercise their right to purchase the property.

3. Tax liens & tax deeds: Don't buy industry/commercial liens unless you've done additional research regarding toxic waste or hazards.

   Laws regarding clean-up on commercial/industry properties are strict. If you ever get a tax lien on commercial property, it converts into a deed and the property requires toxic clean-ups and what not, you the new owner, will be in a serious bind.

   Clean-ups of this kind can easily run into the thousands.

4. Tax liens & tax deeds: The burnt house risk. Some properties are either burnt down or no longer exist, which could be the reason why the property owner is no longer paying for his taxes.

   The property owner may have perished or moved on. For instance, a tax lien on a condo that's already been torn down in Las Vegas would do you no good. You can't rent that out; hence, it is important to research all properties before buying a lien on it by actually seeing it or have someone else view it for you (ie: real estate agent in the area).

5. Tax liens & tax deeds: The ditch. Investing in liens on ditches and sewage retention ponds might not be a good idea—since no one will pay you for it!

    There are some out parcels that have commercial value for outdoor advertising; hence, don't totally knock out parcels out if they are in good view of the highway.

6. Tax liens & tax deeds: The property is in a "bad" part of town. If you want to convert a lien into a deed and make it into a rental property, make sure it's in a neighborhood that people want to live in. Even with the best contractors, a new coat of paint and some curb appeal, if you end up with a property that nobody wants to live in, you're out of luck.

7. Tax deeds: The property is condemned. If you're property has a structure like a house or building, make sure it isn't condemned. What may seem like a good deal might actually be no deal at all. Check with county health and zoning records!

8. Tax liens: Bankruptcy. It has been estimated that in one out of every 200 tax liens purchased, the owner will file bankruptcy on before the end of the redemption period. This is considered relatively a low risk and usually the courts will not shoot down the tax lien. But be mindful of this when you invest, make sure you search property records and figure out if the owners are in bankruptcy proceedings.

9. Tax deeds: Make sure to check with your local zoning and health offices—the property may owe additional fines or "assessments" and as the new owner, you would be the new responsible party.

10. Tax deeds: Check the appraiser's office and visit the property and make sure it isn't a swamp, or a drainage pond. Many counties allow you to view a picture of the property online through various mapping and aerial photography systems. Make sure that even if it's a piece of land that the land is inhabitable and not a breeding ground for alligators and snakes.

Don't Wait!

It's never a good idea to put off researching property until the day before the auction.

Lists given out by counties are sometimes quite long and can take days to find out where properties are located.

Even the most diligent research efforts may not uncover all difficulties or unexpected problems. Therefore be as thorough as possible and always visit the properties long before the auction.

Also utilize the tools the county has provided for you, like free public records sites.

Research Checklist

County governments sometimes give you guides and instructions on how to research properties in their jurisdiction. These can usually be found on the county treasurer or county assessor/appraiser web sites.

The following is a due diligence checklist before going to an auction. This check list is not "universal" and you may need to modify and adjust as necessary depending on the county's rules and regulations.

- ✓ Tax deeds & tax liens: Purchase property in an area you are familiar with. This will eliminate the possibility of you getting stuck with property in a bad neighborhood or a swamp.
- ✓ Tax deeds & tax liens: Research property through the county appraiser's office. This can usually be done online.

By visiting the county appraiser's website, you can search the property by address, owner's name, parcel identification number or lot and block number. The value of the property that the county shows on their appraisal list will generally be from 80 to 85 percent of the fair market value.

✓ Tax deeds & tax liens: Perform a title search on the property.

✓ Tax deeds & tax liens: Title reports, maps, appraisal sheets and tax information are some items that will help you in your research. The county treasurer's office is only a starting point. Sometimes the information available is minimal. It's up to you, as the investor, to pursue other resources.

✓ Tax deeds & tax liens: Ask questions on build-ability, zoning, use restrictions and controls to the appropriate governmental offices. City and county engineering, buildings and codes, and planning departments are good places to get information.

✓ Tax deeds & tax liens: Visit the property sites you are researching! Would you purchase a new home without first inspecting it? Check the property boundaries, if the property has been commandeered by the neighbors for storage or if wildlife has moved in and taken over, will it be worth the time and costs of removal?

✓ Tax deeds & tax liens: You want to make sure you go after properties that do not have waste hazards that you'll be liable for. Or houses that can't be sold back to the market without heavy reconstruction.

✓ Tax deeds & tax liens: Research the genealogy of the property. There may be liens that are from prior tax years that have been purchased by another investor.

✓ Tax deeds & tax liens: You must do all the research! Don't expect the county clerk to do the research for you. Learn your way around the system well before the auction and carry out some practice research so that you'll know what you're looking for when it comes time to research possible investments.

✓ Tax deeds & tax liens: If the property has a mobile home located on it, the sale of the property is usually for the land only. Find out if the mobile home or portable buildings are part of the parcel before bidding on vacant land.

- ✓ Tax deeds: Counties will have files on the property that include information on any other liens, the amount of taxes due, the owner, appraisals and surveys. Some of this information is available online.
- ✓ Tax deeds: Improvements on property aren't always included with the purchase. If a home has an addition built on that wasn't approved by zoning authorities, the addition may have to be taken down before the property can be re-inhabited.
- ✓ Tax deeds: Many parcels have local improvements or special assessments for which payment will be due. Check to find what districts or associations service the parcel you are researching.
- ✓ Tax deeds: Make sure the property you're research doesn't have community or association dues attached to it. Some condos or associations will make improvements, and it's up to the property owner, which would be you, to pay for it, even if you had no say in the plans.
- ✓ Tax deeds: Find out the actual resell value! Go to www.Realtor.com and access the MLS listings in that area to see what parcels are being listed and what price. Call local real estate agents and ask for comparable sales. Always compare!
- ✓ Tax liens: You want to make sure you get paid. So go after liens that are homesteads with people living in them, and that have mortgages on them because banks will pay off liens in worst case scenarios.
- ✓ Tax liens: Perform a bankruptcy search on the property and the property owner. If the property owner filed a bankruptcy within recent years, did they file one which would prevent them from filing before their redemption period runs out? If so, this would be a good investment; they'll either pay you what's due or you can foreclose and sell it.
- ✓ Tax liens: Don't buy small liens unless you know what you're doing. If you purchase a lien for $150, it's probably a vacant lot. While some vacant lots are worth the effort to fork out the money and resale, others are vacant for a reason (ie: flood zone) and the chances of you making enough money from the sale to pay for your hassle will be slim.

Graphical Checklist

Done	Task
✓	Title Search
	Find out value
	Is it a homestead?
	Are there waste hazards?
	Does it need reconstruction?
	Is the area good for resell?
	Research through county appraiser's office
	Perform a bankruptcy search
	Find out about build-ability, zoning and restrictions.
	Will the title company provide a title?
	Any improvements or assessments due?
	Any community or association dues?
	Check property boundaries
	Have others taken over the property?
	What improvements will sell with property?
	Is mobile home or portable building included?
	Check for files on tax deed property
	Find comparable sales in area for tax deeds

Step by Step: Online Tools

You can access most of the information regarding a parcel through county assessor or county appraiser web sites. By using the parcel number provided in the list of properties for sale, you can lookup information such as all previous owners of the property, zoning, property values, taxes, and other relevant data.

Large counties have developed advanced tools online that allow real estate agents, title companies, and investors to look up public record information for free. Smaller counties have contracted their data to third party vendors like qPublic for easy public record lookup.

In the next few pages, you'll learn how to:

- Extract information from InvestingWithoutLosing.com to find out when the next tax auction is.
- How to use NACo's web site to get the contact information and physical address of each county, so you can call them and ask for a list of properties for sale in their tax auctions.
- How to use the county's public records systems to research the properties for sale.

InvestingWithoutLosing.com

You can find out about the latest tax auctions occurring throughout the United States through:
http://www.InvestingWithoutLosing.com

Simply open up your web browser, access the web site, and click on "Upcoming Tax Auctions" link.

NACo Tutorial

SCENARIO: You went on InvestingWithoutLosing.com and found that there is a tax lien sale in Holmes County, FL in June 2007. But you don't know the county information such as their phone number and physical address.

SOLUTION: Access the National Association of Counties (NACo)'s web site at http://www.naco.org and utilize their search engine.

1.) Access www.naco.org

2.) Click on **About Counties** on the top left

3.) Click on **Find Counties** on the drop down menu

4.) Select the state the county is located in.

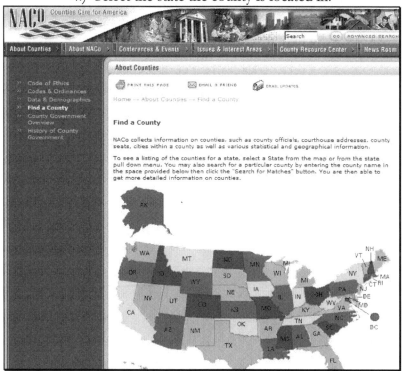

5.) The counties will be listed in alphabetical order. To access the contact information for the county you want, simply click on the link.

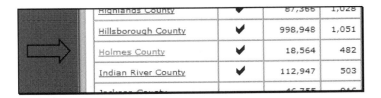

6.) The county's contact information will then be accessible.

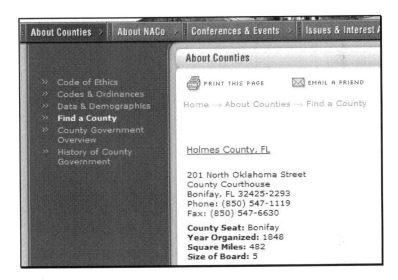

Qpublic Tutorial

Qpublic is one of the more popular tools that counties use for property records search.

Qpublic and its parent company process property record searches all throughout the United States, from Florida to Colorado. Because of their popularity throughout the nation, it's vital that you know how to use Qpublic.

SCENARIO: After finding out Holmes County's phone number through NACo, you contacted them and got a property list. Plus, you found out they have an online lookup tool for property records using Qpublic.

You want to do your due diligence and figure out if there is a property worth bidding on.

SOLUTION: Access Holmes County's public records web site and look up the property records.

PROCESS OF RESEARCHING PROPERTY ONLINE:

1.) Look at the property list and select a parcel that you like to research.

```
13|  ** (0204.00-000-000-012.100      ****|    |     |    Roll Amt    Cert.Amt  |
 |     2005 Final Asamt # R-0030300  HX  |   804|0001|    14.32      22.99 | 18.00|
 | JONES ADDIE NOLA &                25000|    |     | Penalty    Comm     Adv  |
 | PEGGY SUE                             |    |     |    .43      .74     7.50 |
 | 1216 J F JONES RD                     |    |     |                          |
 | GRACEVILLE, FL  32440                 |    |     |                          |
 |                                       |    |     |                          |
 | ORB-0293 P-0502        2.90 AC        |    |     |                          |
 | SEC: 04 TWN: 06 RNG: 13               |    |     |                          |
 | BEG AT NE COR OF SW1/4 OF             |    |     |                          |
 | NW1/4 & RUN E 606' TO POB TH          |    |     |                          |
 | CONT E 234' TH S 188' TH W            |    |     |                          |
 | 234' TH N 188' TO POB DES OR          |    |     |                          |
 | 187/827 DEATH CERT ON FILE            |    |     |                          |
 | FOR A C JONES  OR 225/84 ALSO         |    |     |                          |
 | A PARCEL DES IN OR 292/425            |    |     |                          |
 | OR 293/502 CWD OR 299/851             |    |     |                          |
```

2.) After selecting the parcel number from the property list (0204.00-000-000-012.100), access the Holmes County Public Record/County Appraiser web site on your favorite web browser: http://www.qpublic.net/holmes/

3.) Click on the Property Record Search button on the left hand side of the screen:

4.) Click on **Search by Parcel Number**

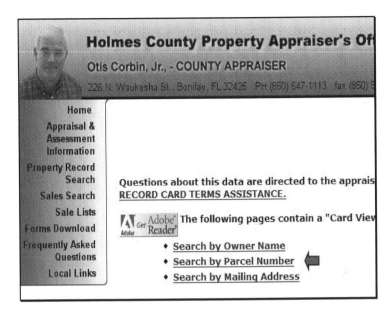

5.) Input our example parcel number: 0204.00-000-000-012.100 in the text box. And then click on the button that says **Search By Parcel ID.**

6.) Information on the property will pop out within a few seconds, giving you a significant amount of data for your due diligence. These data fields can be used for many of the items in the due diligence checklist.

JONES PEGGY SUE		TODAY'S DATE	September 15, 2006
1219 J S JONES RD		PARCEL NUMBER	0204.00-000-000-012.100
		MILLAGE GROUP	COUNTY (1)
GRACEVILLE, FL 32440		TOTAL MILLAGE	17.8110
		PROPERTY USAGE	MOBILE HOME (000200)
	Card View Print		Show Parcel Map

2005 CERTIFIED VALUES

LUE URAL	BUILDING VALUE	TOTAL MISC VALUE	JUST OR CLASSIFIED TOTAL VALUE	ASSESSED VALUE	EXEMPT VALUE	TAXABLE VALUE	HOM STE
0		17,671	26,951	25,804	25,000	804	Y

LAND INFORMATION

NUMBER OF UNITS	UNIT TYPE	SEC-TWN-RNG
2.900	ACRES	04-06-13

BEG AT NE COR OF SW1/4 OF NW1/4 & RUN E 606' TO POB TH CONT E 234' TH S 188' TH W

Show Complete Legal Description

BUILDING DATA

AL EA	HEATED AREA	BED ROOMS	BATHS	PRIMARY EXTERIOR	SECONDARY EXTERIOR	HEATING	COOLING	ACTUA YEA BUIL
		No buildings associated with this parcel.						

MISCELLANEOUS DATA

LENGTH	WIDTH	UNITS	YEAR BUILT
0	0	884 SQUARE FEET	0
0	0	160 SQUARE FEET	0
60	14	840 SQUARE FEET	1970

SALES DATA

NSTRUMENT	QUALIFICATION	IMPROVED? (AT TIME OF SALE)	GRANTOR	GRANTEE
	UNQUALIFIED	YES		PEOPLES BANK OF GRACEV CWD
	UNQUALIFIED	YES		PEOPLES BANK OF GRACEVILLE
	QUALIFIED	NO		JONES A C & ADDIE N & PEGGY
	UNQUALIFIED	YES	2001 CONVERTED JUST VALUE	
	UNQUALIFIED	YES	2001 CONVERTED ASSESSED VALUE	

7.) OPTIONAL: If you click on **Show Parcel Map**, you can also look at the plat map and the aerial photograph of the property as seen below.

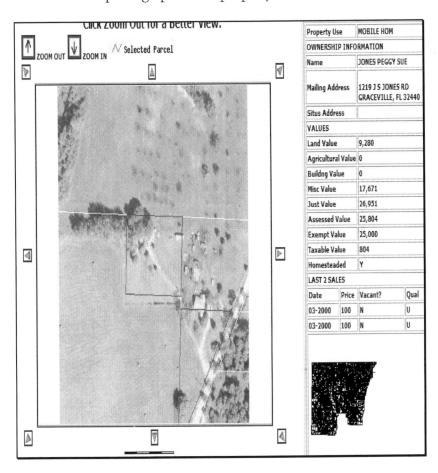

TUTORIAL CONCLUSION: Using some of the data provided online, you found that this tax lien is a homestead (someone living in it). It is zoned residential and for mobile home use. More than likely, this tax lien will be paid off because it's a homestead.

Custom Tools Tutorial

Large counties like Collier County, FL do not use Qpublic but rather have developed their own property record tools online. These online tools vary in size and shape, but they have similar features like Qpublic.

You can search by owner, parcel, and/or address. Additionally, some of these tools are fairly advanced, offering color aerial photography of the properties listed.

Collier County, FL offers color aerial photographs

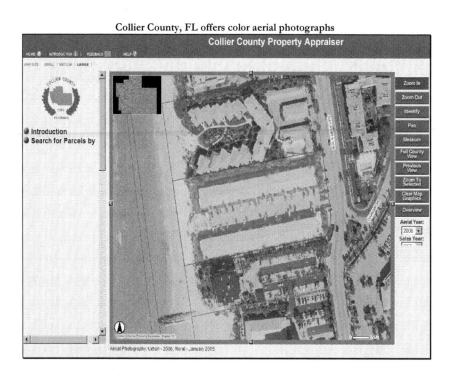

Lee County, FL offers color aerial photographs plus pictures of the structure

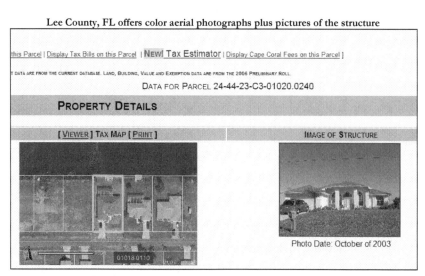

Optional Research Tools

The tools below are for optional use, but many real estate agents and investors use them for research and analysis.

- GPS device
  - o Cost: **$80**
  - o Product Description:
    - ▪ Handheld GPS devices like the Garmin eTrex GPS Unit allow you to know the elevation and GPS coordinates of the properties you're interested in.
    - ▪ Assist in locating future properties.
    - ▪ Helps sell properties easier by allowing potential buyers to know exact locations.
- Google Earth (http://earth.google.com)
  - o Cost: **Free** (advanced versions have fees)
  - o Product Description:
    - ▪ Fly from space to your neighborhood. Type in an address and zoom right in.
    - ▪ Search for schools, parks, restaurants, and hotels. Get driving directions.
    - ▪ Tilt and rotate the view to see 3D terrain and buildings.
    - ▪ Shows topography and GPS coordinates.

Google Earth shows highways, roads, topography

- Trulia.com or Zillow.com
  - Cost: **Free**
  - Product Description:
    - Trends analysis of residential sales in the area
    - Search by price, number of bedrooms, neighborhood and more.

Trulia.com shows sales trends, comparable sales data, etc.

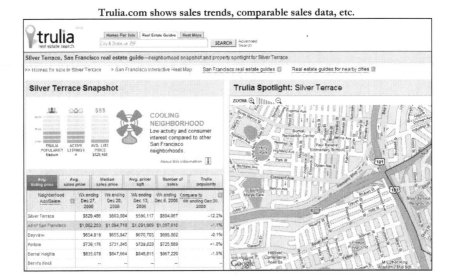

Zillow.com, like Trulia.com, shows sales trends, comparable sales data, etc.

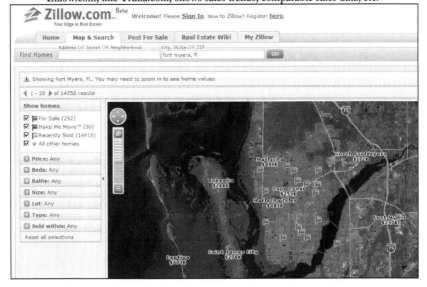

Day 4 Summary

- Start out in your own local jurisdiction so you'll learn how it works.
- Don't venture into other areas until you have an idea of how tax auctions work.
- Through proper due diligence, you can significantly lower your risk; hence, increasing your potential returns.
- Using online tools and web sites like InvestingWithoutLosing.com, NACo, and county public records – you can research most of the properties with ease.
- Online tools like Trulia and Zillow can help you do comparable sales research in the area for free. Google Earth can help you with your GPS coordinates and looking at topography.

"If there's a will, there's a way."

-Anonymous

Day 5: Bidding Types And Strategies

Today you'll learn how to apply certain strategies in auctions and how to bid for short term and/or long term gain. You'll also learn what type of auctions occurs in certain states.

The Bidding Trap

If you've ever bid on auction web sites like eBay, you know there's a certain rush to bidding. In fact, the whole mentality behind bidding is that it goes higher and higher as each bidder is zoned into a mentality that he must win with the highest bid. It's similar to an addiction, you want to avoid the "bidding trap" as much as possible.

Bidding in these auctions is extremely fast paced and it's definitely not for someone that cannot control himself. By conducting proper research, you should already know what the maximum limit is that you can afford for a particular tax lien or tax deed. Don't over bid and don't go with the crowd if they do. Remember, you are in this for a calculated return on your investment; you're not here to gamble your money away.

Too often novice investors come into real estate auctions and overbid each other just because someone hit on their "ego" or "pride" – this will be a downfall if you cannot control yourself. Do not get caught up in the excitement.

Here are some basic rules to follow:
1. Set your budget. Set the maximum amount you want to bid on each property or tax lien before the auction begins. Bidding moves fast and you could be outbid on properties

you really wanted to win. Don't get caught up in the bidding trap. Set your limit and stick to it!

2. Be loud! Do not be shy. There are sometimes dozens if not hundreds of people inside an auction room – bids have been lost because the auctioneer was not able to hear them!

3. Arrive before the sale starts. Scope out your competition but do NOT make arrangements with them on what to bid and what not to bid – this is illegal. Bidding begins at the start of the sale and since some counties have several hundred or even thousands of properties available at each auction, they will begin at the posted time.

4. Consider everyone else's break time your time to rake in the properties. Counties will typically have more than one auctioneer and keep right on with the program during lunchtime and after 5pm when most of the bidders will take a break. Plan ahead so that you can "hang" in there as long as the bidding continues and you may find your competition wavers at those times during the day.

5. Make sure you have made financial arrangements before the auction to take care of whatever properties you purchase. Remember that most counties will only allow 12-24 hours for you to pay for your liens or deeds after the close of the auction, so it's important to secure your funds beforehand, especially if you're working with other investors or you're taking out a loan.

6. Plan your auctions to your advantage. If there is a sale you would like to attend in a small county as well as another in a large county and they're both on the same date, find out if the larger county will be hosting the sale for more than one day. With careful planning you can probably attend both by going to the smaller one and then attending the second day of the larger sale.

   a. You can also use a real estate agent or someone that's knowledgeable in the field to handle your bidding if there are multiple auctions occurring at the same time. You'll need to first ask if the county allows this, and if they do, inquire whether they have recommendations of people that have provided proxy services in the past.

      i. Expect charges ranging from $100 to $300 for proxy services.

ii. Undoubtedly, you want to select someone that is trustworthy and has a good reputation in the area. If you can't get recommendations from the county, you can look for real estate agents by accessing this link: http://www.realtor.org/ Click on the link **Directories** then click on **Find a Realtor**.

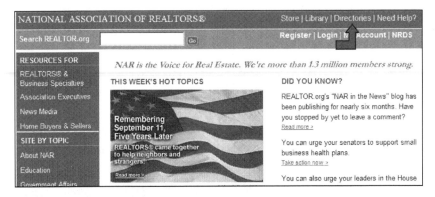

iii. Ask the county if you can overnight a check for the properties that your proxy will bid for. Most counties will understand your situation and will allow you to overnight a check for payment.

iv. Create a list of parcels that you want your proxy to bid on. Create a "cap" for each one of the parcels – signifying the highest you can bid for each parcel. You can then use this to budget for that auction. See the illustration below of what this list should look like.

Proxy Bids	
Parcel Number	Maximum Bid
392010899	$2,993
20991039	$2,349
11390029	$10,981
11839834	$9,201
Location:	Deer Lake County, MI
Auction:	Tax Deed
Proxy Bidder:	John Doe
	Maximum possible charges
	$25,524

Bidding Types for Tax Lien Auctions

As discussed earlier, there are five main bidding types for tax lien auctions. They are as follows:

- Bid down the interest - i.e. Florida's default interest rate on tax liens is 18 percent, but to win it, you have to bid for the lowest interest rate you are willing to accept as a return.

  States like Florida have minimum penalties (usually around 4-5 percent), so even if you bid 0.25 percent interest, you're still getting a minimum rate of return of 4 to 5 percent!

- Premium bidding – you bid above the price for a premium amount. When bidding a premium, the cost of the lien may be $1,000, but the investor purchases the property for $2,000. This means that the lien was $1,000 and the premium is $1,000 making the total due $2,000. The biggest varying factor in this type of bidding is whether you will receive interest on the premiums. In some states you receive interest on tax lien premiums; however, in states like Colorado you do not, in fact it isn't even counted as part of the lien! So be careful when you bid on these –

always check with the county to see if they pay interest on the premium!

- Over the counter – there is no public auction sale. You just go to the county to ask for leftovers from prior years or properties that did not sale or were not paid for after the sale.

- Random selection – the county official will randomly select a bidder and ask if they would like to purchase the property. If they don't want to purchase it, the official will move to the next randomly selected bidder and then find out if anyone wants it. These happen often online.

- Rotational – the county official will go through each bidder and give them the same opportunity to purchase as many liens as the other bidders in the room. The official will start with bidder one and if they make a purchase, they will start the next property with the next bidder, two. This process will continue until all the liens have been purchased.

Bidding Strategies For Tax Lien Auctions

The main bidding strategies for tax lien auctions are as follows:
- Interest on liens strategy - you want to go after tax liens that are likely to be paid back so you can get the interest.
   - Homestead properties, the homes that have people living in them, are the "safest" lien to purchase if you want to make sure it's redeemed.
   - Mortgage companies will usually pay off delinquent taxes – they don't want to lose a $150,000 home on a $1,500 tax lien.
- Lien conversion strategy – you want to go after tax liens that have the highest probability of not being paid. You want to own the property.
   - Out of town owners - If you want to select liens that has a higher probability of not getting paid, select properties that are owned by foreigners or out of state. Some owners have inherited the

property and they have no plans to use it; hence, they give paying taxes on it.

- Small county sale strategy – you want to search for sales in counties that institutional investors will not attend. These are the small counties. Plus, smaller counties equals less competition overall.
  - o Populations of less than 50,000 are considered "small counties" and institutional investors hardly ever participate in these markets. However, just because there aren't a lot of people, that doesn't mean there's no money to be made. Remember, the interest rates stay the same no matter the size of the county's population.
- Small lien strategy – if you are at a sale that's flooded with institutional investors, they usually won't purchase low dollar liens. By purchasing smaller liens, you won't have to compete with their deep pockets. Remember to do your research before purchasing smaller liens so you know you can make a profit.

Bidding Types For Tax Deed Auctions

The most popular bidding types for tax deed auctions are:
- Sealed bids – usually through a sealed envelope and whoever has the highest bid is the winner.
- Public bidding – the highest bidder wins. Some counties start with a minimum bid.

Bidding Strategies For Tax Deed Auctions

- Scope out tax deed auctions that do not have many participants. These may be smaller counties, less publicized auctions, or auctions whose bidders may have been affected by weather problems (ie: hurricane prone Florida).
  - o There are some auctions that take almost an entire day (some even 2-3 days) – some investors leave before the auction ends, which can be costly, as some of the best properties are saved for the last remaining hours.

- Make sure you know how much the property is worth in the market – so you know how much to bid and what your maximum price cap is. You can do this easily by:
    - Researching through recent property sales in the area (available at the county clerk of court or on their web site).
    - Access the real estate listings in the area by going to www.Realtor.com.
- Once you have acquired the property, you can do the following:
    - File a quiet lawsuit to clear the deed and put it on the market (ie: listing it on the MLS). A quiet title is a legal action designed to remove the "clouds" of that title from the previous owners and make sure you have complete ownership of it. Most title companies won't insure tax deeds, except one:
        - A company called Tax Title Services currently offers title insurance without a quiet lawsuit. They insure the following states: Alabama, Georgia, Maryland, South Carolina, California, Illinois, Michigan, Colorado, Indiana, Mississippi, West Virginia, Florida, Louisiana, Missouri, Oklahoma, Tennessee, and New York. For more information, please contact them at (714)371-4041 or access their web site at www.TaxTitleServices.com. With this alternative you can skip the quiet title and market your property.
    - You can sell your property to land wholesalers. LandTrades.com and other similar wholesalers are experienced in clearing the title at their own cost.
    - Sell your property "as is" on auction web sites like Bid4Assets.com or iOffer.com.
    - Keep it for a long term investment. For instance, a prominent ranch family in Southwest Florida bought hundreds of acres of land for pennies on the dollar two decades ago through tax deeds. After twenty years, they sold it to big developers which paid them millions for the property they bought for thousands. Not a bad trade off!

WARNING! Cooperating With Other Bidders

Some investors think it's perfectly legal to have pre-arranged agreement with other bidders so they can purchase tax liens or tax deeds at the lowest cost possible.

These usually happen before the auction, with some people agreeing to not compete with another bidder on select properties.

What many do not know, is that this is a form of bid rigging. An illegal activity defined by the Sherman Act. You could not only potentially lose your bids but your freedom. According to the law, the punishment for this crime is as follows:

> "Shall be punished by fine not exceeding $10,000,000 if a corporation, or, if any other person, $350,000, or by imprisonment not exceeding three years, or by both said punishments, in the discretion of the court."

Day 5 Summary

- There's a number of ways a tax auction is held – bid down the interest, pay over the premium, rotational, and random.
- Make sure you know what type of auction it is before you go into it. Also decide which strategies you are going to apply per parcel. Especially since some states like Colorado do not pay the premium back or they do not pay interest on it.
- You can use proxy bidders to bid for you.
- You can liquidate tax deeds through a variety of methods, from online auction houses to land wholesalers.

"It's tangible, it's solid, it's beautiful. It's artistic, from my standpoint, and I just love real estate."

-Donald Trump

Day 6: Flipping Tax Deeds With Ease

With the advent of the Internet, there are ways to flip properties with ease. On June 30th, 2000, Congress and the President enacted Electronic Signatures in Global and National Commerce Act (ESIGN), which allows businesses and individuals to use electronic signatures (like email) to legally enforce a contract.

In other words, you can complete most transactions online without any need for paper documents. In late 2000, eOriginal in conjunction with Mortgage.com were able to process a paperless mortgage for the purchase of a new home.

What does this mean for you? You can find buyers for your property online, and process your payments online without having to go through traditional real estate brokers/agents.

Once you acquire a deed, you can either keep it for long term or seek to flip it. If you want to flip it, there are several online sites that you can use to sell online: Bid4Assets.com, Craigslist.org, iOffer.com, Overstock.com, and eBay.com.

Bid4Assets.com by far is the favorite real estate auction marketplace online. They specialize in online auctions for high value real estate.

Bid4Assets' community of investors and buyers have attracted sellers across the world, including government agencies selling surplus inventory such as the U.S. Marshals, and the U.S. Department of Treasury.

Flipping With Bid4Assets.com Tutorial

Considered as the "eBay" of real estate properties, Bid4Assets.com allows you to sell your property online securely and easily. Unlike eBay and other auction sites, Bid4Assets cross references your information through a credit bureau when you try to sell for the first time.

This unique verification system is superior to any auction site online and superior to many auctions in the real world because it is a proactive approach in preventing fraud.

The process is FREE and is available to anyone that has a Social Security number. They'll verify items in your credit, your state ID or driver's license, and your birth date, plus since you initiated the query to your credit, it won't appear on your credit report.

Bid4Assets verification system

bid4assets
for serious buyers & sellers

BUY | SELL | REGISTER | MY B4A | EMAIL ALERTS | HELP | SERVICES

Search by: ⦿ Keyword ○ Auction id# [   ] Submit Power Search

★ Sign up for FREE Auction Digest!   ★ U.S. Marshals Service Auctions

> Home > Sell an Asset   Log off

ID Verification   Powered by EQUIFAX

Attention NEW Jewelry/Gem Sellers:
At this time Bid4Assets is accepting only those new jewelry and gem sellers who are both ID verified AND can give evidence of experience as an online and/or business seller in good standing. Please contact service@bid4assets.com to see if your company meets the qualifications for jewelry/gem sellers before you complete the ID Verification process.

To help protect the reputation of our sellers, and to add an extra measure of security for our buyers, we implemented a new ID Verification system that all sellers must pass prior to listing an asset. The process is free and simple, and only takes a couple of minutes to complete. The ID Verification system is secure and does not affect your credit rating. If you have any questions, please click here, or visit our Help section.

Once you're verified, you can then proceed to selling your property by following these instructions:

1. Click on the **SELL** button in the navigation bar.

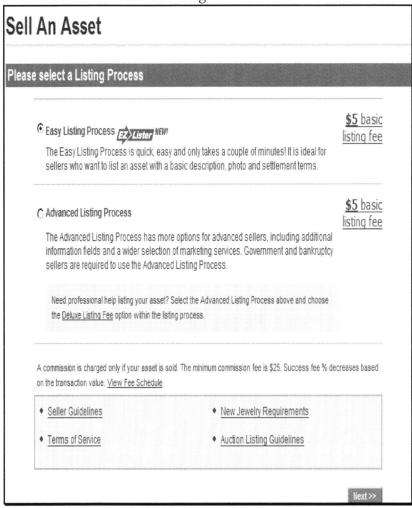

2. Click on **Easy Listing Process** and click **Next >>** on the bottom right.

3. On this page, you'll need to select the category for your property. If it is a house, you'll need to select **Real Estate -> Residential -> Single-Family**. Then you'll need to input a title, like "ARIZONA 3 BEDROOM HOUSE FOR SALE!". Then put in relevant descriptions, terms of settlement, disclosures, and other pertinent information in the large comment box.

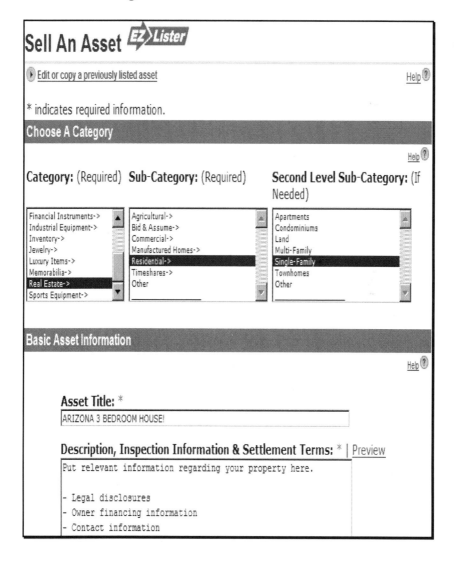

4.   Scroll to the bottom and fill out other pertinent information such as the city, state, and country of where the property is located.

Additionally, upload the images that you've taken of the property, and other points of interest surrounding the property (ie: schools, shopping malls).

Then you'll have to decide when you want to start your auction, either immediate or on a specific schedule. For best results, make sure your auction ends on Saturday, Sunday, or Monday evening, as these are normally when most Internet users are online shopping.

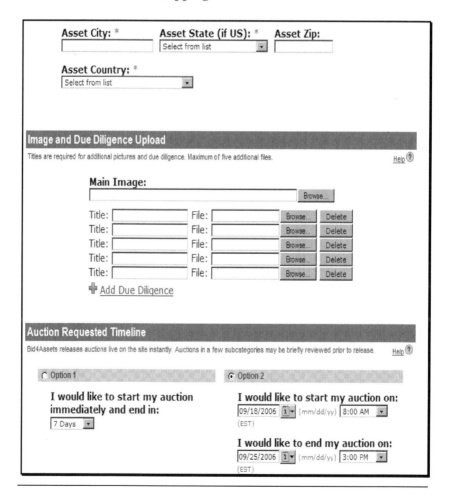

5.   After posting the property details, you'll need to provide Bid4Assets your starting minimum bid (ie: $100.00) and also your credit card number to pay for any listing and final value fees. Their commission structure is as follows:

Transaction Value	Success Fee
$0 - $25,000	10%, plus
$25,001 - $100,000	9%, plus
$100,001 - $200,000	8%, plus
Above $200,000	Contact Bid4Assets

- For all successful auctions, there is a $25 minimum commission fee.
- These fees are cumulative. For example, an asset that sells for $150,000 would have a commission of $13,250.

Final Outlook

Your auction should be easy to read, attractive to look at, and should have the necessary information the buyer needs to make a decision.

Here are some items that need to be in your description:

- Parcel number
- Legal description
- Location (city, state, county)
    - What's nearby? Highways, schools, shops, cinemas.
- Access to electricity and other utilities?
- Homeowner dues or association dues?
- Special assessments by city or county?
- Zoning requirements? (Residential, mobile home, commercial, etc.)
- Type of deed conveyance? (Most common: Warranty or quit claim, see pg. 77)
- Any liens
- Disclosures (Most common: Mold, lead paint)

An example auction that sold on Bid4Assets

Owner Financed Properties

A popular trend among investors selling properties online is to finance the properties. For instance, tax deeds bought for less than $2,000 are being re-sold online for $18,000 or more with owner financing!

It usually involves:
- A low down payment ($500.00 or more)
- No credit checks against the buyer
- A contract agreement that stipulates if the buyer misses at least two payments, he or she will lose all rights to the property and the contract will be voided

The seller can then opt to sell his owner financed loan (private mortgage notes) to note buyers. Note buyers will usually buy loans that have good payment histories and will pay a percentage of the remaining loan (75% to 80% of the value).

Example:

$18,000 owner financed loan
-$2,000 cost of property
-$4,500 note buyer's discount

$11,500 profit (575%)

There are hundreds of note buyers throughout the country. Here are some that are listed on the Internet:

1st United Note Buyers
Lisa Tobert
PO Box 9561
Spokane, WA 99209-9561

BestNoteQuote.Com
American Contract Buyers, LLC
89796 Sea Breeze Dr.
Warrenton, Oregon 97146
1-866-780-2274

PCF Investment Group, Inc.
604 N. 13th St., Suite 8
Rogers, AR 72756
479-986-9158

Anatomy of a Successful Auction

If you want your auction to be successful, you need to follow some basic marketing principles to attract more bids.

- **Your headline needs to be inviting**. Like the auction illustrated above, the headline promises a large home that's near parks and easy access to a freeway. There are hundreds of auctions listed on a daily basis and the first thing everyone reads is the headline. If you can't attract them with a good headline, potential bidders won't click on your auction.

- **Your follow-up.** After the headline, there needs to be an immediate call to action in the body of your description. You've seen these on TV – companies innovatively will offer a special offer if they are one of the first one hundred callers in the next 20 minutes.
- **Let the buyer picture himself with the property.** Let the buyer imagine what it would be like to own the land or the home. Talk about the area, the benefits of the community, rental potential and vacancy rates, etc.
- **Have a good reputation.** On almost all auction sites, there are feedback or rating systems for buyers and sellers. This tells potential customers how many transactions you've conducted and whether it went smoothly. If your feedback or rating is less than satisfactory, you'll see diminished sales. Consequently, if you have no feedback or rating at all, buyers are less inclined to buy from you.
  - **Tip:** If you have a handful of items that you are planning to buy in the future, whether it's toothpaste or your next bundle of printer paper, consider buying it online on the auction site you're going to sell on. You can build your feedback!
- **Photos and your copy text.** Pictures ARE worth a thousand words. Don't under estimate the power of pictures and its ability to sell. Additionally, your copy text should be believable, sincere, truthful, and exciting.

BAD: The house is 3 bedrooms, 2 baths. It has carpet and has a patio. There's a lake that you can see from it.

GOOD: Imagine yourself relaxing in this luxurious 3 bedroom, 2 baths, carpeted home – with a lake view that can be seen directly from the patio!

Deed Conveyance

After your auction and you've received your payment from your buyer, you'll need to convey a real estate deed to transfer ownership of the property.

Real estate deeds are recorded at your local clerk of courts/county recorder's office. You can either convey your deed with warranties, or you can convey it without warranties. If your deed is conveyed without warranties and is sold "as is", your auction may have less bids as it isn't as attractive.

Here are the most common types of deeds conveyed:

1. **General warranty deed**. A warranty deed guarantees that the seller is the clear title holder of the property, and he can sell it to a prospective buyer. The seller also promises to protect the buyer against any title defects.

Additionally, if another person were to try to claim the property down the road, the warranty deed would legally protect the buyer and the buyer would be entitled to compensation from the original seller.

2. **Quit claim deed**. Quit claim deeds are legal documents by which a seller releases or "quits" any rights they have to a property. The quit claim has the least assurance to the buyer as it has no warranties.

Most tax deeds are quit claim deeds, in that they are conveyed and sold "as is" with no guarantees or warranties. It is up to you, the seller, to issue a warranty or a quit claim deed when you are transferring your property.

If you purchased title insurance for your tax deed, and you are confident that there are no faults in the property, you could convey your property as a warranty deed to the new owners.

If you don't want to hassle with guarantees and want to sell your property as is, then you can use the quit claim route.

WARRANTY DEED SAMPLE

For good consideration, I the grantor, JOHN DOE of 555 TART LN, BATTLE CREEK, MI 20932, County of Delat State of Michigan, hereby bargain, deed and convey to JANE WOE of 3333 MARY AVE, LAYFIELD, MD 32901, County of RELISH, State of MARYLAND, the following described land in DELAT COUNTY, free and clear with WARRANTY COVENANTS; to wit:

RANDOM PROPERTY UNIT 5, BLOCK 10, LOT 1

Grantor, for itself and its heirs, hereby covenants with Grantee, its heirs, and assigns, that Grantor is lawfully seized in fee simple of the above-described premises; that it has a good right to convey; that the premises are free from all encumbrances; that Grantor and its heirs, and all persons acquiring any interest in the property granted, through or for Grantor, will, on demand of Grantee, or its heirs or assigns, and at the expense of Grantee, its heirs or assigns, execute and instrument necessary for the further assurance of the title to the premises that may be reasonably required; and that Grantor and its heirs will forever warrant and defend all of the property so granted to Grantee, its heirs, against every person lawfully claiming the same or any part thereof.

Being the same property conveyed to the Grantors by deed of OCTOBER 20, 2006.

WITNESS the hands and seal of said Grantors this 20th day of OCTOBER, 2006.

Grantor: _____

Grantee: _____

STATE OF _____

COUNTY OF _____

On_____before me,_____, personally appeared _____, personally known to me (or proved to me on the basis of satisfactory evidence) to be the person(s) whose name(s) is/are subscribed to the within instrument and acknowledged to me that he/she/they executed the same in his/her/their authorized capacity(ies), and that by his/her/their signature(s) on the instrument the person(s), or the entity upon behalf of which the person(s) acted, executed the instrument.

WITNESS my hand and official seal.

Signature:_____

QUITCLAIM DEED SAMPLE

THIS QUITCLAIM DEED, Executed this 20th day of October, 2006, by first party JOHN DOE whose post office address is 555 TART LN, BATTLE CREEK, MI 20932 to second party, JANE WOE, whose post office address is 3333 MARY AVE, LAYFIELD, MD 32901.

WITNESSETH, That the said first party, for good consideration and for the sum of $50.00 paid by the said second party, the receipt whereof is hereby acknowledged, does hereby remise, release and quitclaim unto the said second party forever, all the right, title, interest and claim which the said first party has in and to the following described parcel of land, and improvements and appurtenances thereto in the County of Delat, State of Wyoming, to wit:

RANDOM PROPERTY UNIT 5, BLOCK 10, LOT 1

IN WITNESS WHEREOF, The said first party has signed and sealed these presents the day and year first above written.

Signed, sealed and delivered in presence of:

_____   _____
Witness   First Party

_____   _____
Witness   Second Party

STATE OF   }
COUNTY OF   }

On_____before
me,_____, personally
appeared_____,
personally known to me (or proved to me on the basis of satisfactory evidence) to be the person(s) whose name(s) is/are subscribed to the within instrument and acknowledged to me that he/she/they executed the same in his/her/their authorized capacity(ies), and that by his/her/their signature(s) on the instrument the person(s), or the entity upon behalf of which the person(s) acted, executed the instrument.

WITNESS my hand and official seal.

_____
Signature

Real Estate Attorneys

It's important to have good legal advice, especially if you are a beginner in selling properties. Before you start selling properties on your own, make sure you are in compliance with applicable local, state, and federal law.

Attorneys can consult with you; review your documents, contracts, and give you an assessment of potential risks. When you speak to an attorney, make sure you speak to someone that specializes in real estate law. Get recommendations from local real estate agents and don't be afraid to ask for someone's credentials.

Taxes and Good Recordkeeping

It's important to note that you need to make sure you keep track of your sales and consider your potential taxes based on your profits.

Flipping properties can give you profits immediately; however, it would be prudent to save a portion of your profit to offset taxes. Keep good records of any improvements and associated costs for each property as they may be tax deductible – which is good news for those that want to offset their taxes.

Please talk to a professional tax consultant on these matters to save you from headaches. Additionally, there's an ample amount of resources online that provide tax advice, such as Bankrate.com. Here are some articles that you may want to read up on:

> Home sweet homeownership tax breaks
> By Kay Bell
> http://www.bankrate.com/brm/itax/news/20030207a1.asp
>
> Tax consequences of flipping real estate
> By Kay Bell
> http://www.bankrate.com/brm/news/tax/20050922a1.asp
>
> Tax-deductible home remodeling
> By George Saenz
> http://www.bankrate.com/brm/itax/tax_adviser/20041007a1.asp

Day 6 Summary

- Auction sites like Bid4Assets, iOffer, Overstock, and eBay allow you to sell properties quickly online.
- Successful auctions have imaginative headlines, images, and copy text.
- You could opt to sell your property with owner financing and profit even further by selling your note to a note buyer.
- After the auction, you can convey your property through two types of deeds: warranty or quit claim.
- It's advisable to seek legal advice if you're selling on your own for the first time.
- Make sure to speak with a CPA or tax consultant about your investments and keep good records of any improvements on any property as it might be tax deductible.

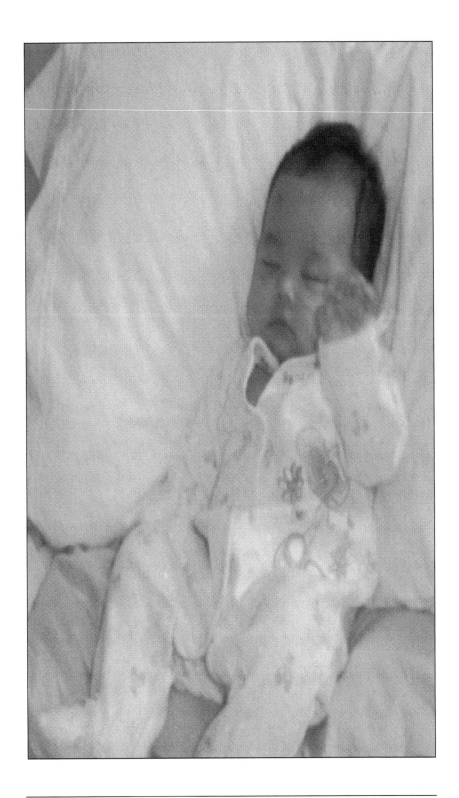

"Remember the Sabbath day by keeping it holy. Six days you shall labor and do all your work, but the seventh day is a Sabbath to the LORD your God. On it you shall not do any work..."
-God

Day 7: Conclusion

It's the end of the week and you've read through a lot. This particular day is designed to highlight what an investor should do on the seventh day – rest.

Over 40% of people report they perform better when they come back from resting or vacationing.

One of the gravest mistakes an investor can do is spending money without a clear mind. You need to be on your best performance when you come to a real estate auction. Get well rested from the day prior, make sure you have your notes and strategies ready. And even if you've done this a hundred times, don't slack off -- consider each time as if it was your first.

The second gravest mistake you can do in this venture is ignoring family and friends due to work. Don't forget why you are investing: it is for your livelihood and your family's well-being.

Why does it matter when you become a millionaire only to find your family doesn't know you? Who is truly successful, the man with the billions but with three failed marriages, or the one that's earning a middle income salary with a family that smiles?

Surprise your spouse, treat your children to a family activity, go fishing --- do something else aside from investing and work. Designate a rest day! And if anyone argues otherwise, tell them it's even handwritten in the Ten Commandments!

Never Stop Learning

There are various resources online and in print about tax auctions. Several books cover state law in greater detail and have more in-depth analysis of state statutes. Additionally, some topics like 1031 Exchanges (which are rare for tax deeds), might be useful to you down the road when you accumulate enough properties in your portfolio.

Here are some suggested in-print reading:

>   **Profit by Investing in Real Estate Tax Liens: Earn Safe, Secured, and Fixed Returns Every Time**
>   By Larry Loftis
>   ISBN: 0793195179
>
>   **Selling Real Estate without Paying Taxes**
>   by Richard T. Williamson
>   ISBN: 0793167981

Online resources:

>   **InvestingWithoutLosing.com:** This book's web site, which gives you access to times/dates of future tax auctions.
>
>   **BankRate.com:** Great resource online for investment and real estate articles as well as calculators.
>
>   **http://members.cox.net/manoil/:** Arizona Tax Lien information.

About the Author

Don Sausa is the Vice President of LandTrades.com, a premier online provider of vacation and investment properties. He is the author of the *Investing Without Losing* book series, an array of books that cover investment topics such as real estate and investing strategies.

An active real estate investor, Sausa has personally bought tax liens throughout the United States and has experience in acquiring properties from institutions, government agencies, and local governments. He has bid on properties owned by individuals, corporations, mortgage companies, banks, and even properties owned by the United States.

Sausa is also an experienced technical writer. He has written thousands of knowledge base articles, security advisories, training curriculums, and instruction manuals for companies like BellSouth, Teleperformance USA, and Team Asylum. His work has been featured on television such as ABC7 News and has been published in newspapers, online forums and industry magazines such as Garnett's News-Press, MSNBC.com, LA Times, and the Industry Standard.

Rio Grande Gorge in Taos, New Mexico.

References

ABC (2000). *Thief sues property owner for injuries.* Retrieved 2006 from ABC News, Web site: http://abcnews.go.com/US/wireStory?id=2065474

Flagler County (2002). *Ground Rules for Tax Deed Sale For Florida Counties.* Retrieved 2006 from Florida Statute, Web site: http://clerk.co.flagler.fl.us/taxdeed_rules.html

Heath, Samantha (2001). *Electronic Signatures in Global and National Commerce Act.* Retrieved 2006 from Department of Commerce, National Telecommunications and Information Administration Web site: http://www.ntia.doc.gov/ntiahome/ntiageneral/esign/comments/eoriginal.htm

Johnson, Tory (2006). *The Death of the American Vacation.* Retrieved 2006 from ABC News, Web site: http://abcnews.go.com/GMA/Careers/story?id=2151399&page=1

Leonard, Justin (2006). *Uncensored infomercial complaints.* Retrieved 2006 from Web site: http://www.infomercialscams.com/

Manoil, Mark (2002). *Arizona Property Tax Lien Primer.* Retrieved 2006 from Web site: http://members.cox.net/manoil/objects/atlprmr.PDF

Richards, Malcolm (2005). *Priority of mortgage and tax liens.* Retrieved 2006 from Texas A&M University, Real Estate Center Web site: https://www.recenter.tamu.edu/pdf/1110.pdf#search=%22120%20days%20IRS%20tax%20lien%22

Sausa, Don (2006). *Investing Without Losing.* ISBN 0978834623 and ISBN 0978834607

Weiss, Philip (2000). *The Lives They Lived: Fred C. Trump.* Retrieved 2006 from NY Times, Web site: http://query.nytimes.com/gst/fullpage.html?res=9A02E2D91E39F931A35752C0A9669C8B63&sec=&pagewanted=3

Wiki (2006). *FICO score.* Retrieved 2006 from Wikipedia, Web site: http://en.wikipedia.org/wiki/Credit_score

Glossary

abatement
A reduction or decrease.
The removal of a nuisance.

abstract of title
A summary or digest of all transfers, conveyances, legal proceedings, and any other facts relied on as evidence of title, showing continuity of ownership, together with any other elements of record which may impair title.

acceleration clause
A condition in a real estate financing instrument giving the lender the power to declare all sums owing lender immediately due and payable upon the happening of an event, such as sale of the property, or a delinquency in the repayment of the note.

access right
The right of an owner to have ingress and egress to and from owner's property over adjoining property.

acre
A measure of land equaling 160 square rods, or 4,840 square yards, or 43,560 square feet, or a tract about 208.71 feet square.

adjustable rate mortgage
A mortgage loan which bears interest at a rate subject to change during the term of the loan, predetermined or otherwise.

ad valorem
A Latin phrase meaning 'according to value'. Usually used in connection with real estate taxation.

affiant
One who makes an affidavit or gives evidence.

affidavit of title
A statement, in writing, made under oath by seller or grantor, acknowledged before a Notary Public in which the affiant identifies himself or herself and affiant's marital status certifying that since the examination of title on the contract date there are no judgments, bankruptcies or divorces, no unrecorded deeds, contracts, unpaid repairs or improvements or defects of title known to affiant and that affiant is in possession of the property.

agent
One who acts for and with authority from another called the principal.

agreement
An exchange of promises, a mutual understanding or arrangement; a contract.

angel investors
A person who provides backing to very early-stage businesses or business concepts. Angel investors are typically entrepreneurs who have become wealthy, often in technology-related industries.

appraisal
An estimate of the value of property resulting from an analysis of facts about the property. An opinion of value.

appraiser
One qualified by education, training and experience who is hired to estimate the value of real and personal property based on experience, judgment, facts, and use of formal appraisal processes.

appreciation
The increase in the value of a property due to changes in market conditions, inflation, or other causes.

appropriation of water
The taking, impounding or diversion of water flowing on the public domain from its natural course and the application of the water to some beneficial use personal and exclusive to the appropriator.

appurtenance
That which belongs to something, but not immemorially; all those rights, privileges, and improvements which belong to and pass with the transfer of the property, but which are not necessarily a part of the actual property. Appurtenances to real property pass with the real property to which they are appurtenant, unless a contrary intention is manifested. Typical appurtenances are rights-of-way, easements, water rights, and any property improvements.

assessor
A public official who establishes the value of a property for taxation purposes. Similar to county appraiser.

bankruptcy
By filing in federal bankruptcy court, an individual or individuals can restructure or relieve themselves of debts and liabilities. Bankruptcies are of various types, but the most common for an individual seem to be a "Chapter 7 No Asset" bankruptcy which relieves the borrower of most types of debts. A borrower cannot usually qualify for an "A" paper loan for a period of two years after the bankruptcy has been discharged and requires the re-establishment of an ability to repay debt.

chain of title
An analysis of the transfers of title to a piece of property over the years.

clear title
A title that is free of liens or legal questions as to ownership of the property.

cloud on title
Any conditions revealed by a title search that adversely affect the title to real estate. Usually clouds on title cannot be removed except by deed, release, or court action.

collateral
In most loans, a real estate property is the collateral. The borrower risks losing the property if the loan is not repaid according to the terms of the loan.

county appraiser
See *assessor.*

county clerk
See *recorder.*

credit rating
A credit rating is an evaluation of the likelihood of a borrower to default on a loan.

equity
The difference between the market value of a property and the claims held against it.

fair market value
The highest price that a buyer, willing but not compelled to buy, would pay, and the lowest a seller, willing but not compelled to sell, would accept.

fee simple
The greatest possible interest a person can have in real estate.

FICO score
FICO is a credit score scale used by many mortgage lenders that use a risk-based system to determine the possibility that the borrower may default on financial obligations to the mortgage lender.

foreclosure
The legal process by which a borrower in default under a mortgage is deprived of his or her interest in the mortgaged property. This usually involves a forced sale of the property at public auction with the proceeds of the sale being applied to the mortgage debt.

grantee
The person to whom an interest in real property is conveyed.

grantor
The person conveying an interest in real property.

interest rate
A rate which is charged or paid for the use of money.

IRA
Individual Retirement Account. One of several specific retirement accounts allowed by the IRS to provide tax-deferral or other tax advantage.

legal description
A property description, recognized by law, that is sufficient to locate and identify the property without oral testimony.

lender
A term which can refer to the institution making the loan or to the individual representing the firm. For example, loan officers are often referred to as "lenders."

liability insurance
Insurance coverage that offers protection against claims alleging that a property owner's negligence or inappropriate action resulted in bodily injury or property damage to another party. It is usually part of a homeowner's insurance policy.

lien
A legal claim against a property that must be paid off when the property is sold. A mortgage or first trust deed is considered a lien.

lien conversion
See *foreclosure*.

line of credit
An agreement by a commercial bank or other financial institution to extend credit up to a certain amount for a certain time to a specified borrower.

liquid asset
A cash asset or an asset that is easily converted into cash.

mortgage
A legal document that pledges a property to the lender as security for payment of a debt. Instead of mortgages, some states use First Trust Deeds.

note
A legal document that obligates a borrower to repay a mortgage loan at a stated interest rate during a specified period of time.

note buyer
Someone that purchases notes at a discount.

owner financing
A property purchase transaction in which the property seller provides all or part of the financing.

public auction
A meeting in an announced public location to sell property.

quit claim deed
A deed that transfers without warranty whatever interest or title a grantor may have at the time the conveyance is made.

quiet title suit
A lawsuit filed to ascertain the legal rights of an owner to a certain parcel of property.

real estate agent
A person licensed to negotiate and transact the sale of real estate.

real property
Land and appurtenances, including anything of a permanent nature such as structures, trees, minerals, and the interest, benefits, and inherent rights thereof.

Realtor®
A real estate agent, broker or an associate who holds active membership in a local real estate board that is affiliated with the National Association of Realtors.

recorder
The public official who keeps records of transactions that affect real property in the area. Sometimes known as a "Registrar of Deeds" or "County Clerk."

recording
The noting in the registrar's office of the details of a properly executed legal document, such as a deed, a mortgage note, a

satisfaction of mortgage, or an extension of mortgage, thereby making it a part of the public record.

redemption

After a period of time expires called the redemption period, investors, often for only the taxes, penalties and interest due, can purchase the property.

tax deed

A deed on property issued when the property is purchased at a public sale for nonpayment of taxes.

tax lien

A type of lien placed on a title when the owner has not paid property or assessment taxes or other state and federal taxes.

title insurance

Insurance that protects the lender (lender's policy) or the buyer (owner's policy) against loss arising from disputes over ownership of a property.

title search

A check of the title records to ensure that the seller is the legal owner of the property and that there are no liens or other claims outstanding.

zoning

Regulations that control the use of land within a jurisdiction.

Index

Appendix A

Tax Calendar

State	Schedule	Contact
Alabama	May/June	(251) 943-5061
Alaska	April/May	(907) 269-8600
Arizona	February	(602) 506-8511
Arkansas	Varies by county	(870) 946-4321
California	Varies by county	(510) 272-6347
Colorado	November	(303) 654-6100
Connecticut	Varies by county	(860) 742-7305
Delaware	Varies by county	(302) 744-2300
Florida	May/June	(352) 374-5210
Georgia	Varies by county	(912) 632-5214
Hawaii	Varies by county	(808) 961-8211
Idaho	Varies by county	(208) 253-4561
Illinois	November	(217) 277-2150
Indiana	August/September/October	(260) 724-2600
Iowa	June	(641) 322-3240
Kansas	Varies by county	(620) 365-1407
Kentucky	Varies by county	(270) 384-2801
Louisiana	Varies by county	(337) 788-8800
Maine	Varies by county	(207) 784-8390
Maryland	Varies by county	(301) 777-5911
Massachusetts	Varies by county	(508) 362-2511
Michigan	October	(517) 627-3211
Minnesota	April/May, September/October	(218) 927-7283
Mississippi	August	(601) 442-2431
Missouri	August	(660) 665-3350
Montana	Varies by county	(406) 563-4000
Nebraska	March	(402) 461-7132
Nevada	Varies by county	(775) 887-2100
New Hampshire	Varies by county	(603) 524-3579
New Jersey	Varies by county	(609) 343-2201
New Mexico	Varies by county	(505) 768-4000
New York	April, August	(518) 447-7300
North Carolina	December	(336) 228-1312
North Dakota	November	(701) 845-8500
Ohio	Varies by county	(330) 297-3889
Oklahoma	Varies by county	(580) 223-8414
Oregon	Varies by county	(541) 523-8200

Pennsylvania	September	(717) 337-9820
Rhode Island	Varies by county	(401) 421-7740
South Carolina	October/November	(803) 584-3438
South Dakota	Varies by county	(605) 773-3311
Tennessee	Varies by county	(931) 484-6165
Texas	Varies by county	(903) 723-7432
Utah	May	(435) 734-3300
Vermont	Varies by county	(802) 388-7741
Virginia	Varies by county	(757) 787-5700
Washington	Varies by county	(509) 659-3236
West Virginia	October/November	(304) 457-3952
Wisconsin	September	(715) 395-1568
Wyoming	July/August/September/October	(307) 721-2541

Redemption Periods

State	Type	Bid Type	Over the Counter	Interest Rates	Period of Redemption
Alabama	Lien	Premium/Yes		12% annum	3 years
Alaska	Deed	Varies/Yes		N/A	1 year
Arizona	Lien	Bid Down/Yes		16% annum	3-5 years
Arkansas	Deed	Premium/No		N/A	30 days
California	Deed	Premium/No		N/A	N/A
Colorado	Lien	Premium/Varies		Varies	3 years
Connecticut	Deed Hybrid	Premium/No		18% annum	1 year
Delaware	Deed Hybrid	Premium/No		15% penalty	60 days
Florida	Lien	Bid Down/No Liens but Deeds Sold		18% down to 5% min.	2 years
Georgia	Deed Hybrid	Premium/No		20% penalty	1 year
Hawaii	Deed Hybrid	Premium/No		12% annum	1 year
Idaho	Deed	Premium/No		N/A	N/A
Illinois	Lien	Bid Down/No		18% penalty	2-3 years
Indiana	Lien	Premium/No		10-15% penalty	1 year
Iowa	Lien	Rotates/No		24% annum	2 years
Kansas	Deed	Premium/No		N/A	N/A
Kentucky	Lien	Premium/No		12% annum	1 year
Louisiana	Deed Hybrid	Bid Down/No		12% annum + 5% penalty	3 years
Maine	Deed	Sealed/No		N/A	N/A
Maryland	Lien	Premium/Yes		6-24% annum	6 months
Massachusetts	Deed Hybrid	Premium/No		16% annum	6 months
Michigan	Deed	Premium/No		N/A	N/A
Minnesota	Deed	Premium/Yes		N/A	N/A
Mississippi	Lien	Premium/Yes		18% annum on lien	2 years
Missouri	Lien	Premium/No		10% annum + 8% on further	2 years

			taxes	
Montana	Lien	Rotates/Yes	10% annum + 2% penalty	3 years
Nebraska	Lien	Rotates/Yes	14% annum	3 years
Nevada	Deed	Premium/No	N/A	N/A
New Hampshire	Deed	Premium/No	N/A	N/A
New Jersey	Lien	Bid Down on Premium/No	18% annum	2 years
New Mexico	Deed	Premium/No	N/A	N/A
New York	Deed	Premium/No	N/A	N/A
North Carolina	Deed	Premium/No	N/A	N/A
North Dakota	Lien	Premium/No	12% annum	3 years
Ohio	Deed and Lien	Premium/No	18% annum for lien	3 years for lien
Oklahoma	Lien	Rotates/Yes	8%	2 years
Oregon	Deed	Premium/Varies	N/A	N/A
Pennsylvania	Deed Hybrid/ Varies by property	Premium/Varies	10% when applicable	1 year when applicable
Rhode Island	Deed Hybrid	Premium/No	10% penalty + 1% penalty a month starting with 7th month	1 year
South Carolina	Lien	Premium/Yes	8-12% annum	1 year
South Dakota	Lien	Premium/Yes	12% annum	3 years
Tennessee	Deed Hybrid	Premium/No	10% annum	1 year
Texas	Deed Hybrid	Premium/Varies	25% penalty	6 months – 2 years
Utah	Deed	Premium/No	N/A	N/A
Vermont	Lien	Varies by Town/Varies by Town	12% annum	1 year
Virginia	Deed	Premium/No	N/A	N/A
Washington	Deed	Premium/No	N/A	N/A
West Virginia	Lien	Premium/No Liens but Deeds Sold	12% annum	17 months
Wisconsin	Deed	Premium & Sealed/No	N/A	N/A
Wyoming	Lien	Rotates/Yes	15% annum + 3% penalty	4 years

Appendix B

Sample tax certificate

TREASURER'S OFFICE COSTILLA COUNTY   STATE OF COLORADO

𝔗𝔞𝔵 𝔏𝔦𝔢𝔫 𝔖𝔞𝔩𝔢 ℭ𝔢𝔯𝔱𝔦𝔣𝔦𝔠𝔞𝔱𝔢 𝔬𝔣 𝔓𝔲𝔯𝔠𝔥𝔞𝔰𝔢

No.   Book
43755   40

Tax Lien Sale Certificate of Purchase

LORRAINE C. MEDINA

COUNTY TREASURER
TO
SALSA WORLDWIDE LLC

ISSUED DECEMBER 01, A.D.2005

, A.D. 20

FOR VALUE RECEIVED, I hereby assign the within Certificate, and all my right, title and interest to the property therein described, to

_____

_____

_____

This Certificate surrendered and

$ .... redemption money paid to

_____

.... , A.D. 20 ....

By ....
County Treasurer / Deputy

.... , A.D. 20 ......

This Certificate surrendered and deed made

to ....

_____

By ....
County Treasurer / Deputy

I HEREBY CERTIFY, That a Tax Lien Sale of Real Estate, situate in the County of COSTILLA COUNTY State of Colorado for Delinquent Taxes for the year 2004 at the County Treasurer's office in the County aforesaid, on DECEMBER 1, 2005 in accordance with the law, SALSA WORLDWIDE LLC was the Purchaser(s) of the Tract hereinafter described, as having been sold, for which the Purchaser(s) paid the sum of money set opposite the caption "Total paid" for Certificate, being the amount of Taxes on the whole of said estate for which the purchaser(s) is to receive interest until redemption at the maximum statutory rate".

YEAR	SCHEDULE NUMBER	NAME OF OWNER WHEN KNOWN
2004	70245810	KOURAKIS VASSILLIOS IOANNIS

DESCRIPTION OF PROPERTY

S.D.C.R. UNIT 1 BLK 123 LOT 1995
CONT 5.191 AC(WD 315-117)

ASSESSED VALUE   1015

COSTS	
TAXES	
INTEREST	
ADVERTISING	
CTF FEE	
TOTAL	
PREMIUM BID	

14.0 % per ann
14.0 % st of is
12.0 % per ann

RECORD

YEAR	DA PAID
20	
20	
20	
20	
20	
20	
20	
20	
20	

In Witness When
1ST DA
LORRAINE
By _____
Certificate No.

Sample tax deed

83-337-1260

No delinquent taxes and transfer entered;

Certificate of Real Estate Value

( )filed (X)not required

February 6, 2006

Sharon K. Andersen

By _____ County Auditor

_____, Deputy

This deed transfers real property in exchange for $500 or less of consideration.

A000509611

OFFICE OF COUNTY RECORDER
CASS COUNTY MINNESOTA

CERTIFIED, FILED, AND/OR
RECORDED ON
02/06/2006   04:14:55PM

AS DOC #:   A000509611
PAGES: 1
REC FEES: $46.00

KATHRYN M. NORBY
COUNTY RECORDER

BY _____
DEPUTY

Conveyance of Forfeited Lands

Issued Pursuant To Minnesota Statutes, Sections 282.01 to 282.12 inclusive, as amended.

Commissioner's Deed No. 0201299

THIS DEED, Made this 3rd day of February, 2006, by and between the State of Minnesota, acting by and through the Commissioner of Revenue (Grantor), and Sausa Worldwide LLC, A Florida Limited Liability Company (Grantee), WITNESSETH:

WHEREAS, the land hereinafter described, having been duly forfeited to the State of Minnesota for the nonpayment of taxes, was sold under the provisions of Minnesota Statutes, Sections 282.01 to 282.12, inclusive, to the Grantee, and,

WHEREAS, the Grantee has paid in full the purchase price of said land and has otherwise fully complied with the conditions of said sale and is entitled to an appropriate conveyance thereof,

NOW, THEREFORE, the State of Minnesota, pursuant to said statutes, and in consideration of the premises, does hereby grant and convey without warranty unto the Grantee, Forever, the following described land lying and being in the County of Cass, and State of Minnesota, to-wit:

Lots 15 thru 18, Block 12
Original Plat, City of Bena,

excepting and reserving to the said state, in trust for taxing districts concerned, all minerals and mineral rights, as provided by law.

TO HAVE AND TO HOLD THE SAME, together with all the hereditaments and appurtenances thereunto belonging or in anywise appertaining.

THE GRANTOR CERTIFIES that the Grantor does not know of any wells on the described real property. The State of Minnesota is issuing this deed for the county and other taxing jurisdictions and in reliance on the Auditor's certification stating no wells are located on the above described property.

IN TESTIMONY WHEREOF, the State of Minnesota has caused this deed to be executed in its name in the City of St. Paul, County of Ramsey and State of Minnesota, the day and year first above written.

STATE OF MINNESOTA)
) ss.
County of Ramsey   )

On this 3rd day of February, 2006, before me personally appeared ALAN G. WHIPPLE, the duly appointed representative of the Commissioner of Revenue of the State of Minnesota, to me known to be the person who executed the foregoing conveyance in behalf of the State of Minnesota and acknowledged that he executed the same as the free act and deed of said state pursuant to the statutes in such case made and provided.

LINDA F. LEITOLD
Notary Public-Minnesota
My Commission Expires Jan 31, 2010

STATE OF MINNESOTA
DANIEL A. SALOMONE
Commissioner of Revenue

By: _____

THIS INSTRUMENT WAS DRAFTED BY:

Minnesota Department of Revenue
600 North Robert Street, 4th Floor
St. Paul, MN 55146

Tax statements for the real property described in this document should be sent to:

Mission Statement

We aim to introduce you to new alternative investments, because having little or no control of your money stinks. For instance, when you pick a mutual fund you aren't calling the shots on where your money is going. But with tax auctions, you decide where your money goes!

Archives

10/01/2006 - 10/31/2006
11/01/2006 - 11/30/2006

Contact Author

Upcoming Auctions This Month!

Wednesday, November 22, 2006

There are more real estate auctions coming this month. These are not necessarily based on tax liens or tax deeds but by other federal govt agencies.

2+ ACRES OF COMMERCIAL LAND
FM544 & Heritage Parkway, Murphy, Texas 75074
Auction: Tuesday, November 28, 2006
Total Site Area: 2.189 ± acres
Description: Land located at the Northwest corner of FM544 and Heritage Parkway in Collin County. Zoned Commercial D4 with public utilities available.

For more info, click here.

Example inquiry letter or fax to county treasurer

December 00, 2007

County Treasurer

133 Street Ave

Joetown, USA 00000

Dear County Treasurer:

I would like to request information regarding your upcoming tax lien or tax deed sales this year. Would you kindly provide me the contact information of the newspaper you are publishing your tax sales in? Additionally, please provide the location and dates of your tax sales.

You can contact me by fax through xxx-xxx-xxxx or you can mail it back to me using the self-addressed, stamped envelope I have included.

Thank you,

Joe Investor

Phone: (xxx) xxx-xxxx

Email: joe@investor.com

Sample of a foreclosure notice

NOTICE OF FORECLOSURE SALE NOTICE OF PUBLIC AUCTION FORECLOSURE SALE: Residential Property Location: 661 California St. Stratford CT Pursuant to a judgment of the Superior Court for the Judicial District of Fairfield at Bridgeport in: Bank of New York vs. Robert Butler et al Docket No.: FBT CV 06 5003026 S 03 the above identified property will be sold subject to Court approval at public auction on Saturday December 2 2006 at 12:00 Noon on the premises. SUBJECT TO "CONDITIONS OF ALL SALES" LISTED ON THIS PAGE. The property will be sold as a whole "as is" without representations of any kind free and clear of the interest of the parties bound by said judgment but subject to taxes and such other liens and encumbrances not foreclosed by said judgment subject to tenants in possession and subject to all laws ordinances or governmental restrictions and subject to easements and restriction appearing of record if any. The property will be open for inspection from 10:00 am to 12:00 Noon on the date of sale. The successful bidder shall deposit with the committee at the time of the sale a certified or bank check in the amount of Twenty-Eight Thousand Five Hundred Dollars ($28,500.00). The balance of the purchase price is to be paid upon the passing of the committee deed which must take place not later than Thirty (30) days from the approval of said sale by the Court. If the purchaser is unable to complete the sale within said Thirty (30) day period the deposit shall be forfeited. Further description of the property and further particulars of the terms of the sale as ordered by the Court may be obtained from the court file or from the committee. RUSSELL G. SMALL COMMITTEE 135 ELM STREET BRIDGEPORT CT 06604 TELEPHONE - (203) 368-6173 FACSIMILE - (203) 368-6176

Sample of tax deed application notice in Florida

(Investor converting tax lien to tax deed.)

NOTICE OF APPLICATION FOR TAX DEED

NOTICE IS HEREBY GIVEN THAT HANSEL & PHILIP PRESCOTT holder of the following Tax Sale Certificate has filed said Tax Certificate for the Tax Deed to be issued thereon. The Certificate Number and year of Issuance, the Description of property, and Name(s) in which it is assessed is as follows:

Certificate Number: 40

Year of Issuance: 1998

Description of Property: ALL BLK 3, HAROLD Parcel ID: 19-2N-26-1660-00300-0010 Name in which Assessed: --

All of the above property is located in Santa Rosa County, In the State of Florida.

Unless such certificate shall be redeemed according to Law, the Property described in such Certificate will be sold to the Highest Bidder, at the east end lobby of the County A d m i n i s t r a t i v e Complex at 6495 Caroline St., Milton, Florida on the 16th day May, 2005 at 12:00 noon.

Dated this the 23th day March, 2005. Mary M. Johnson Clerk of the Circuit Court of Santa Rosa County, Florida

Sample of ROI calculation for tax liens

ROI calculator you can use to calculate tax lien rate of returns.
Available from http://www.pine-grove.com/Web%20Calculators/roi.htm.

Return on Investment (ROI) Calculator

Amount Invested?:	$0.00
Start Date? (m/d/y):	12 / 06 / 2006
Amount Returned?:	$0.00
End Date? (m/d/y):	12 / 06 / 2007
Gain or Loss:	$0.00
Percentage Gain or Loss:	0.0000%
Annualized Return:	0.0000%
Total Years:	0

Calc   Clear   Print   Help

financial calculators (c) 2006 Pine Grove Software, All rights reserved.

Sample of over the counter tax deeds in Lee County, FL

COUNTY OF LEE - CHARLIE GREEn, CLERK

DELINQUENT TAX SALE REPORT

REPORT DATE: 01/26/2006 1:37:36 pm

LANDS AVAILABLE

For The Sale Dates Beginning 1/6/1997 to 1/26/2006

12/07/1999

TD #: 1999505958   Legal Description: 100 FT FPL EASMENT SEC 19 PER OR 475 PG 32 OR 0220 PG 0210

STRAP: 19452700000000010   OPENING BID: $21,821.43

OWNER: WEST COAST TURNAROUND INC

1 Total Deeds

Sample of Smith County, TX tax sale notice – instructing investors their tax sales are handled by law firms and not by the county.

SMITH COUNTY DOES NOT SELL TAX LIEN CERTIFICATES

INVESTORS MAY PURCHASE PROPERTIES AT OUR TAX SALES OR BY SEALED BID AFTER THE PROPERTY HAS BEEN "STRUCK OFF".

★ TAX SALE INFORMATION ★

REQUIRMENT: Completed written statement of no taxes due from the Smith County Tax Assessor-Collector's office.

DATE AND TIME: First Tuesday of every month at 10:00 a.m.

LOCATION: West steps of the Smith County Courthouse located at 100 N. Broadway in Tyler, Texas.

TO OBTAIN A TAX SALE LIST: The tax attorney's website at www.publicans.com and www.pbfcm.com. In the Tyler Morning Telegraph on three occasions prior to sale during the two weeks preceding the sale (dates vary). Notices are also posted at the Smith County Courthouse.

PAYMENT: Payment in full is required of the winning bidder on the day of sale. Payment must be by cashier's check, personal check, or cash. Credit cards are not accepted.

OTHER COSTS: The other costs that must be paid at time of sale are: any fees that have not been paid, other costs associated with the sale; also, taxes for post judgment years may also be due from the buyer.

DEED: A sheriff's deed is issued at the time of sale, or shortly thereafter.

REDEMPTION: The owner may redeem the property at any time up to six months to two years after the sale. The redemption period varies for each property according to the type of property, the length of time we have been trustees, etc. When an owner redeems the property, he must pay the investor the amount paid at time of sale plus 25% and any costs of sale during the first year of redemption. During the second year, the investor is entitled to the amount paid at the time of sale plus 50% and any costs of sale.

Sample of federal government selling foreclosed properties and tax deeds.
Source: http://app1.sba.gov/pfsales/dsp_search.html

Property For Sale

SBA

- About
- Search
- All Property
- Comments
- SBA Offices

State Summary

Click Here For Region Summary

Last Modified:

Region	Comm.	Res.	Farm	Mach.	Vacant	Other	Sub-total
AK	1	0	0	0	0	0	1
CO	0	1	0	0	0	0	1
IA	1	0	0	0	0	0	1
IL	0	0	0	0	1	0	1
MT	1	0	0	0	0	0	1
PA	2	0	0	0	0	0	2
Total	5	1	0	0	1	0	7

Last Modified: Text Version

* The structure of this page was last modified. 02/26/2002 07.18.42 AM
Version. 1.2.0

RESIDENTIAL LOT - ONLINE AUCTION

960 Micheltorena Street, Los Angeles, CA 90026

Online Auction: December 11-13, 2006

Total Site Area: 3,720 ± sq. ft.

Description: Hillside lot that slopes down from the street and has views of the canyon and Los Angeles skyline (shown in photo). Public utilities are available and the lot has paved access. The land is located in Los Angeles County and is zoned LAR2. Minimum bid updated on 11/13/06.

For complete details on this property click on the photo or CLICK HERE

SINGLE FAMILY HOME ON 9 ± ACRES

2670 Moores Mill Road, Spencer, Virginia 24165

Auction: Tuesday, December 12, 2006

Total Living Space: 1,571 ± sq. ft.

Description: 3 bedroom, 2 bath home overlooking the Mayo River. Amenities include vaulted ceilings, wrap-around deck, and fireplace. The property sits on 9 ± acres with river access and private picnic area.

For complete details on this property click on the photo or CLICK HERE

Sample of U.S. Marshals Foreclosured Properties For Sale
Source: http://www.usdoj.gov/marshals/assets/sales.htm

United States Marshals Service
Justice   Integrity   Service   "America's Star."

U.S. Marshals Service >> Asset Forfeiture Program >> Current Asset Sales

Current Asset Sales

Updated 12-01-06	A General List of Auctions in December 2006 - Specific information on assets that are scheduled for auction.

The assets listed below are on the auction block on Bid4Assets web site. Click on the link to view details.

Amarillo, TX - 300 S. Maryland Street

Auction Dates: December 04 – December 06, 2006

Bedford, NY - Single Family Residence Situated on 20.21 Acres of Land

Auction Dates: December 04 – December 06, 2006

Piedmont, MO - Single Family Home Located on 201.68 +/- Acres of Land

Auction Dates: December 04 – December 06, 2006

Prospect, CT - Single Family Home

Auction Dates: December 05 – December 07, 2006

North Branch, MI - 3222 North Branch Road

Auction Dates: December 11 – December 13, 2006

Brought to you by the Participating Newspapers of America

The public notice database on this site is not a substitute for the official publication that is required by law. You will still find those notices in your local newspaper.

All Across America, Public Notices are your 'Right To Know'

A single database of Public Notices -- which you may know as "Legal Ads" -- has been created by newspapers in a number of states.

Legislatures require many kinds of public notices so you stay informed about government, corporate and private activities that touch your world. Now newspapers that publish them have enhanced the legislative intent and made them available in one place, any time you need it.

Delivered to your Email Address

Word search the database manually at no charge, or subscribe to Public Notice Smart Search and have Notices important to you or your company sent to your email address automatically.

Public Notices from eight states are in the database (search each state separately). Just click a link below to get to that state.

Alabama	Georgia	Maryland	New Jersey (75,136*)	South Carolina
Alaska	Hawaii	Massachusetts (2*)	New Mexico	South Dakota
Arizona (81,156*)	Idaho	Michigan (57,496*)	New York	Tennessee
Arkansas	Illinois	Minnesota	North Carolina	Texas
California	Indiana	Mississippi (4,565*)	North Dakota	Utah
Colorado	Iowa (13,858*)	Missouri	Ohio (29,676*)	Vermont (*)
Connecticut (*)	Kansas	Montana (5*)	Oklahoma	Virginia (15,803*)
Delaware	Kentucky	Nebraska	Oregon (5,250*)	Washington
District of Columbia	Louisiana (5,532*)	Nevada	Pennsylvania	West Virginia
Florida	Maine (*)	New Hampshire (*)	Rhode Island (*)	Wisconsin

Sample of FDIC foreclosure deed sales
Source: http://www.fdic.gov/buying/owned/index.html

Sample of private investment group selling tax foreclosed properties at a discount

Source: http://www.atfs.com/

MAKING THE DIFFERENCE IN LOCAL COMMUNITIES

NEWS | GOVERNMENTS | INVESTORS | TAX LIENS FOR SALE | REAL ESTATE FOR SALE | TAXPAYERS | CONTACT

Real Estate Sales

Overview

The properties you see listed on this website were acquired by ATF through tax certificate foreclosure. We offer these properties at prices below market value, and as such, they can be a very attractive investment.

There are a few things to consider before deciding to submit an offer for one of our properties. All our properties are sold on an "as is" basis regarding the physical condition of the property and occupancy of the property. We do not provide financing and transactions are expected to close within 30 days of our acceptance of an offer. A minimum 10% deposit is required (in some cases more) which is non-refundable upon the execution of a contract. Because the specific circumstances affecting each property are unique, we will be happy to answer any questions you may have. Just follow the appropriate link or call the phone number listed for each property.

Property Listings

- Properties in CT
- Properties in NJ
- Properties in SC
- Properties in FL
- Properties in KY
- Properties in OH
- Properties in IN

American Tax Funding

For questions regarding available real estate, contact **(877) SELL REO**

Sample FDIC selling foreclosed properties.

Source: http://www.resales.usda.gov/

 United States Department of Agriculture   Real Estate For Sale

Search

Rural Development
○ Single Family Housing
○ Multi Family Housing
○ Business - Cooperative

Farm Service Agency
○ Farm/Ranch

Advanced Search

Rural Development
○ Single Family Housing
○ Multi Family Housing
○ Business - Cooperative

Farm Service Agency
○ Farm/Ranch

Rural Development Real Estate for Sale

 Single Family Housing real estate for sale includes government owned real estate and potential foreclosure sales for single family homes.

 Multi Family Housing real estate for sale includes government owned real estate and potential foreclosure sales for Multi family housing.

 Business and Cooperative Programs real estate for sale includes government owned real estate and potential foreclosure sales for houses, lots, buildings, machinery, and equipment.

Farm Service Agency Real Estate for Sale

 Farm Loan Program real estate for sale includes government owned real estate and potential foreclosure sales for farm/ranch properties, houses, lots, and buildings.

Over the counter Mississippi land sales

http://lands.sos.state.ms.us/tfl/index.asp

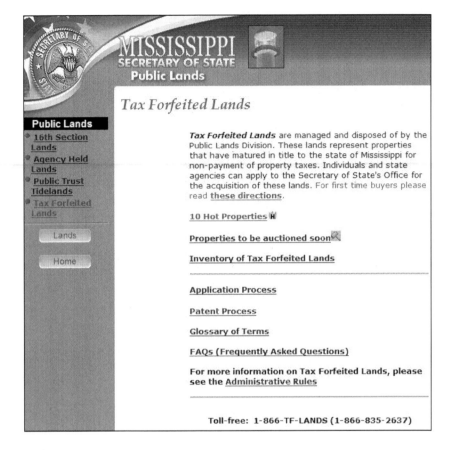

Tax Forfeited Lands

Public Lands

- 16th Section Lands
- Agency Held Lands
- Public Trust Tidelands
- Tax Forfeited Lands

[Lands]

[Home]

Tax Forfeited Lands are managed and disposed of by the Public Lands Division. These lands represent properties that have matured in title to the state of Mississippi for non-payment of property taxes. Individuals and state agencies can apply to the Secretary of State's Office for the acquisition of these lands. For first time buyers please read **these directions**.

10 Hot Properties

Properties to be auctioned soon

Inventory of Tax Forfeited Lands

Application Process

Patent Process

Glossary of Terms

FAQs (Frequently Asked Questions)

For more information on Tax Forfeited Lands, please see the Administrative Rules

Toll-free: 1-866-TF-LANDS (1-866-835-2637)

Investing Without Losing
ORDER FORM

Your book is printed on paperback cover. If you wish to order a **hardcover** version of this book, please check below.

___Complete Guide to Real Estate Tax Liens and Foreclosure Deeds: Learn in 7 Days—Investing Without Losing Series (**$29.95**)

We have several books coming out soon, if you wish to pre-order this, you can get 10% off the cover price plus free shipping within the U.S. Please check below.

___Investing Without Losing: Lending To Strangers With Interest Securely (**$17.95**)

___Investing Without Losing: Savings Bonds (**$17.95**)

Mail your check or credit card, name, address, zip, telephone, and email to:

The Vision Press
690029 Daniels Pkwy #147
Fort Myers, FL 33912
support@thevisionpress.com

NOTE: If your book is damaged or out of date, no matter where you bought it from, you can trade it in. Just send in $15.00 and the front cover --- and we'll send you the completely updated brand new edition!

The Vision Press
FEEDBACK

The Vision Press would like to hear from you! We invite our readers to send us constructive feedback regarding our published books. If we utilize your feedback, we'll send you a free copy of any future editions!

Send your feedback to: support@thevisionpress.com

Please include your name, email address, mailing address, and the book you are giving feedback on.

[tvp]

Made in the USA
San Bernardino, CA
10 May 2015